Essentials of Leadership in Africa

This concise overview of the theories and practice of leadership in the African context is the first of its kind. *Essentials of Leadership in Africa* introduces leadership as an art and science to inspire confidence and support among the people who need to achieve common organisational goals. We present a framework of leadership which emphasises the role of the African context in better understanding leadership effectiveness. According to our model, leadership in Africa can be understood by focusing on the leader's skills, motives, and behaviours; the leader's role in developing teamwork and team leadership; and the organisational context. It is important to understand that leadership does not occur in a vacuum. Each chapter includes illustrative real-life examples, experiential exercises, short cases, and/or assessments.

The book appeals to undergraduate and graduate students in Africa and/or other parts of the world who are interested in leadership on the African continent. In addition, managers, trainers, and practitioners can benefit from reading *Essentials of Leadership in Africa.*

Bella L. Galperin is Dana Professor at the J.H. Sykes College of Business, The University of Tampa.

Caren B. Scheepers is Professor at the Gordon Institute of Business Science, University of Pretoria.

Essentials of Business and Management in Africa
Series Editors: Bella L. Galperin, Terri Lituchy, Betty Jane Punnett and Ali Taleb

This series of shortform textbooks offers a range of books which focus on the essentials of various aspects of business and management in the African context.

In focusing on the core elements of each sub-discipline, the books provide a useful alternative or supplement to traditional textbooks, and can be used by trainers and managers as well. Each book provides information on basic concepts in the sub-discipline and examples to illustrate how these concepts are affected by the African context.

Essentials of General Management in Africa
Betty Jane Punnett and Lemayon Lemilia Melyoki

Essentials of Organisational Behaviour in Africa
Betty Jane Punnett and Thomas Anyanje Senaji

Essentials of Leadership in Africa
Bella L. Galperin and Caren B. Scheepers

For more information about this series, please visit: www.routledge.com/Essentials-of-Business-and-Management-in-Africa/book-series/EBMA

Essentials of Leadership in Africa

Bella L. Galperin and
Caren B. Scheepers

Routledge
Taylor & Francis Group
NEW YORK AND LONDON

First published 2025
by Routledge
605 Third Avenue, New York, NY 10158

and by Routledge
4 Park Square, Milton Park, Abingdon, Oxon, OX14 4RN

Routledge is an imprint of the Taylor & Francis Group, an informa business

ISBN: 978-0-367-43520-2 (hbk)
ISBN: 978-1-032-90686-7 (pbk)
ISBN: 978-1-003-02052-3 (ebk)

DOI: 10.4324/9781003020523

Typeset in Sabon
by SPi Technologies India Pvt Ltd (Straive)

Bella L. Galperin
To my parents, Colpan and Samuel, who instilled in me a passion for the pursuit of knowledge. To my husband, Daniel, for his continued support in helping me achieve my dreams. To my children, Lev and Liam, who inspire me to make the world a better place.

Caren B. Scheepers
To my parents, Danie and Isobelle Jooste, my in-laws, Ds. Dawie and Margaret Scheepers, who encouraged my service to the world and who instilled Christian values in me. To my husband, Marius, for his unwavering consistent support and who, together with my children, Darius and Clarisse, has supported my quest to make a difference in and for Africa.

Contents

Figures

Tables

Authors

Dr. Bella L. Galperin is Dana Professor in the Management and Entrepreneurship Department in the J.H. Sykes College of Business at The University of Tampa. She is also Senior Associate Director of TECO Energy Center for Leadership. She has published numerous peer-reviewed journal articles and book chapters in the areas of leadership, workplace deviance, and cross-cultural management. She also co-authored a book titled *LEAD: Leadership Effectiveness in Africa and the African Diaspora*. She is a board member of The Sustany Foundation and has worked as a consultant in the telecommunications, pharmaceutical, and clothing industries.

Dr. Caren B. Scheepers is Professor at the University of Pretoria's Gordon Institute of Business Science (GIBS). She teaches in the domain of contextual strategic leadership, entrepreneurial leadership, diversity, equity, and inclusion. She published 50 case studies, 40 local and international academic articles, and authored, co-authored, and co-edited seven peer-reviewed books. She is a professional executive coach and counselling psychologist and has extensive corporate and entrepreneurial experience as an organisational development consultant and executive coach.

1 Overview of leadership in Africa

Chapter summary

This chapter provides a contextual background for the remaining chapters and develops a framework for the entire book. We discuss the importance of studying leadership and its central role in driving change in Africa. The chapter begins by defining leadership and how it differs from management. We also discuss the key leadership roles and how leadership can be learned. Finally, the chapter discusses the African continent from geographic, historical, economic, and cultural perspectives and their impacts on leadership.

Learning objectives

After studying this chapter, you should be able to do the following:

- Recognise the importance of studying leadership today and its key role in driving change in Africa.
- Define the meaning of leadership and how it differs from management.
- Discuss the leadership roles.
- Understand that leadership can be learned.
- Identify the African contextual factors influencing leadership.

Ory Okolloh, a Johannesburg-based Kenyan lawyer in her thirties, along with four young bloggers from Kenya, launched the website called Ushahidi (Ushahidi.com). Ushahidi is a communication forum that allows anyone to report cases of violence through text message, e-mail, or web submission and to portray the information on an online map. According to a study by Harvard University scholars, Ushahidi has been the most comprehensive tool in gathering crisis-related information in Kenya (Meier & Brodock, 2008). Ushahidi was also used to monitor the

DOI: 10.4324/9781003020523-1

2009 India general elections and organise snow removal during a massive snowstorm in Washington, DC. The software also collected data during the COVID-19 global pandemic.

Okolloh and her start-up venture illustrate how young African leaders developed a software which is now used in different parts of the globe. The scenario also highlights key distinctions between leadership and management. That is, leadership produces change. Conversely, management focuses on order and consistency. Okolloh is just an example of many young leaders in Africa. While there is a commonly held belief that Africa lacks leaders, a study found that young leaders do exist but they are often "invisible at the table, in the spaces and at the levels that matter" (African Leadership Institute, 2018: 1).

Our introductory chapter discusses the meaning of leadership and how it differs from management. We also provide an overview of the leadership approaches across time. The chapter then examines the various roles performed by leaders and how leadership can be learned. We finally discuss the overall environment in Africa and how contextual factors influence the leadership process.

The importance of leadership

Given the uncertainty and rapid changes in today's business environment, challenges continue to arise; organisations need effective leadership to be able to respond to those challenges with intelligence, strategy, and expertise. Organisational success requires flexible leaders who can skilfully lead through change, attain organisational goals, increase performance, and cultivate a people-first culture of engagement and accountability.

Leadership is the art and science to inspire confidence and support among the people who need to achieve common organisational goals. By motivating people towards a shared vision, leaders can provide the direction to achieve the goals and objectives of the team. Leaders influence the attitudes and behaviours of their staff. Great leaders are not only comfortable in their own roles and in their ability to accomplish their jobs, but they also communicate well with their team members and mentor their employees. Leaders provide support to their subordinates, so they can do their jobs and meet their own goals. Great leaders challenge their staff and hold them accountable, but they also take responsibility if the team fails at something.

The question remains – why are there so few great leaders? According to Seth Godin, "Leadership is scarce because few people are willing to go through the discomfort required to lead" (Goodreads, 2003). Brené Brown, an American professor, author, and podcaster, further explains that this scarcity makes leadership valuable. In general, it is uncomfortable to challenge the status quo and resist the urge to settle for less. When leaders feel comfortable, it's unlikely that they are experiencing their full potential (Goodreads, 2003). When managers do not challenge the status quo, it does not mean that they are incapable of leadership. Rather, it is an indication that they are not receiving the guidance needed to be placed in leadership roles. Managers must be provided with the information on how to strengthen the goals of their organisations. Furthermore, managers need to develop their skills and abilities so that they can contribute to organisational effectiveness. By providing individuals with the needed training, they will be more likely to attain the organisational goals.

Through leadership skill development, managers can learn how to create a vision for their team and inspire others. In organisations, leaders are needed to guide teams. When teams are leaderless, teams become indecisive, disorganised, and fragmented. Ethical lapses are more likely to occur, and there is often a lack of vision. First, leaders empower their teams to make important decisions. Also, leaders help the team make timely decisions. Second, leaders facilitate the communication in teams which can assist with organising the team. Third, leaders can also help with bringing the team together and making the team more cohesive. Fourth, leaders can also build the values and behaviours of the team to ensure the team's integrity. Finally, leaders have a vision of the collective goals of the organisation and ensure that the team is accomplishing them (Eades, 2023).

While some may argue that Africa lacks leadership (Eckert & Rweyongoza, 2020), Africa has traditionally been the cradle of great leadership. Many African leaders are well known around the world—including Nelson Mandela, Kwame Nkrumah, Steve Biko, and Julius Nyerere, to name a few. Africa's contribution to leadership philosophy has also been remarkable. Two examples include: Africa was the birthplace of *Ubuntu*, a Nguni Bantu term meaning "humanity", and translated as "I am because we are". *Ubuntu* is the belief in a universal bond of sharing that connects all humanity—similarly, *Umoja*, a Kiswahili word, meaning unity and togetherness. Africa also gave rise to *Satyagraha*, a Sanskrit word meaning "truth," which is the notion of passive resistance, which Gandhi developed when he lived in Africa. Both these terms are known around the world. Today, the demand for effective leadership and systematic leadership development in Africa is growing more rapidly than ever before. A critical shortage of upcoming leaders is responsible for the underdevelopment of organisations in many African countries (Ugwuegbu, 2001); they are underperforming compared to their potential and could improve their performance by strengthening their leadership. Now that we have covered the importance of leadership, we expand on the meaning of leadership.

Leadership defined

What is leadership? There are multiple definitions of leadership in the literature. Since leadership means different things to different people, there are almost as many definitions of leadership as there are people who have tried to define the word (Stogdill, 1974). A Google search of "What is leadership" can provide 945,000,000 results. In the book, *The Future Leader*, Jacob Morgan (2020) interviewed some of the world's top CEOs and asked them to define leadership. Table 1.1 lists some of the leadership definitions provided. We define **leadership** as the ability to inspire confidence and support among the people who are needed to achieve organisational goals (Kim & Maubourgne, 1992).

Table 1.1 CEOs' definitions for leadership

CEOs' quotes for definitions of leadership
Leadership is about helping others realise their potential and inspiring them to work with you to achieve a shared vision for the future. — Kathy Mazzarelli, CEO, Graybar
Ensuring that people have everything they need to achieve the missions of an organisation. That's it, all else is footnotes. — Hans Vestburg, CEO, Verizon Communications
Leadership is a combination of legitimacy, personality and management skills that make others want to follow someone's direction. — Pierre-André de Chalendar, CEO, Saint Gobain
Leadership is helping people succeed, inspiring and uniting people behind a common purpose and then being accountable. — Paul Polman, Former CEO, Unilever
A leader focuses on both the vision of the future and the possibility and the hard realities of the present and the lessons learned of the past, a person who inspires others, someone who is a walking symbol of humility. — Bernard Tyson, Former CEO, Kaiser Permanente
As a leader you must trust and empower your teams. Give them a clear direction, explain the purpose of the company and give them the means to do their jobs. A leader must also empower people and help them grow and build on their strengths while practicing to improve on their blind spots. — Isabelle Kocher, Former CEO, Engie
Leadership is showing up and stepping up at a time when people need you and doing the right thing, no matter how hard it is. I remember my former boss said to me that there's a right thing to do and there's an easy thing to do, and very rarely is the right thing to do the easy thing to do. — Keith Barr, Former CEO, InterContinental Hotels Group

(*Continued*)

Table 1.1 (Continued)

CEOs' quotes for definitions of leadership
Leadership is about the ability to drive results, set the vision and share it, create an environment of success, and remove obstacles. — Judy Marks, CEO, Otis Elevator
A leader is someone who can think strategically, simplify the strategy so everyone in the organisation can understand it and communicate that strategy simply, enthusiastically, and in a caring way. — Ajay Banga, CEO, MasterCard
The most basic definition of leadership is you set the destination. You come up with a strategy to get to that destination and do your best to align and supply the resources to make that happen. — Mark Hurd, Former CEO, Oracle
Leadership is helping believe in a better tomorrow or a better outcome than you have today. — Marissa Mayer, Former CEO, Yahoo!
Make setting audacious goals a fundamental belief. Do things, as John F. Kennedy famously said, "not because they are easy, because they are hard." Leadership stands for progress, empowerment, empathy and trust. At a time of too many cynics who throw up their hands and cry, "impossible," I employ optimism, the only free stimulus in this world. — Bill McDermott, CEO, ServiceNow; Former CEO, SAP
Leadership is getting people to willingly go someplace they wouldn't go themselves. — Tom Wilson, CEO, Allstate
I define leadership as making a positive impact on people; employees, shareholders, customers, business partners and the public at large. — Levent Çakiroglu, CEO, KOC Holdings
Leaders must paint a picture of a common future you are working towards. This entails not only getting people to understand what that future looks like, but also to participate in the painting of the picture; buying into it and committing to it. — Fani Titi, Group CEO, Investec Financial Services Group, an Anglo-South African banking and wealth management group
For me, leadership is the responsibility to create the right conditions for individuals from different backgrounds and with complementary skills to work together, find solutions, and create robust plans. — Neal Froneman, CEO, Sibanya-Stilwater Mining Group headquartered in South Africa
We need to tap the right leadership. We need inspirational leadership that is not selfish, but instead service oriented. — James Mworia, CEO, Centum Investment Company Limited, public East African investment company headquartered in Kenya

Source: Morgan (2020), Oberholster (2023), and Mulupi (2012).

Most leadership definitions agree upon the following elements:

1 Leadership is a group phenomenon. Leadership occurs when a person influences or persuades a group of individuals. Leadership is an interpersonal process. There are no leaders without followers.

2 Leadership is about achieving organisational common outcomes. Leadership is a process to which a person influences a group to achieve a common goal. Leadership is goal-oriented and can play a part in the life of a group, tribe or community.
3 Leadership is about influence.
4 Leadership is a process of social influence between and among many sources of leadership including the leader, followers, and context. There are many mechanisms that can impact the process, such as leader's and followers' traits, behaviours, and emotions.

How does leadership differ from management?

To understand leadership, one must understand the differences between leadership and management. While leadership focuses on influencing, motivating, inspiring, creating, and mentoring, the key functions of management are planning, organising, directing (or leading), and controlling (Mintzberg, 2009). **Management** is defined as the attainment of organisational goals effectively and efficiently through planning, organising, staffing, directing, and controlling organisational resources.

The key differences between leadership and management are as follows:

Leadership is about **creating** a vision and strategy and shared culture of values, maximising opportunity, and keeping an eye on the horizon. Leadership focuses on building a culture of agility, honesty, and trust. Management is about planning and budgeting, minimising risk, focusing on the bottom line, maintaining stability, and creating a culture of efficiency.

Leadership is **motivating** others to learn by providing learning opportunities and stressing networking and flexibility. Management is the emphasis on organising, staffing, directing, controlling, and creating structure and order.

Leadership is about investing in people – **influencing** and **inspiring** subordinates with purpose and trust. Management focuses on the investment of goods, use of position power, and the emphasis on the achievement of subordinates' goals.

Leadership is about **mentoring** and coaching and the emphasis on listening and building connections. Management is about maintaining emotional distance, imparting information, and providing insights into the organisation. Table 1.2 lists some of the differences between leadership and management.

Table 1.2 Differences between leadership and management

Leadership	*Management*
Creating	Planning
Motivating	Organising
Influencing	Staffing
Inspiring	Directing (leading)
Mentoring	Controlling

Source: Based on Mintzberg (2009).

While leading can be a large part of a manager's job, a manager must conduct other functions (e.g., planning, organising and controlling). Effective leaders must be good managers or supported by effective managers. Both leaders and managers need to communicate, make decisions, and solve problems (O'Leary, 2016). In the scenario at the beginning of the chapter, Okolloh produced change and acted as a leader by launching Ushahidi, the new website. Nevertheless, she also needed to pay bills and taxes on time. Effective leaders also manage and effective managers also lead. Okolloh was largely focused on leadership; hence, the difference between leadership and management is also about the weight placed on its respective functions.

Overview of approaches across time

Over the decades, there has been an evolution of leadership approaches. In the early 1900s, definitions of leadership focused on control and centralisation of power with a focus on domination (Moore, 1927). The **Great Man theories**, the earliest theories of leadership, viewed leaders (traditionally thought of as males) as individuals born with certain heroic leadership traits and natural abilities for power and influence. During the 1920s, leadership began to be defined in terms of the leader's traits, emphasising their capacity for influence rather than domination. In general, **trait theories** examine whether leaders possess certain traits or characteristics that increase success compared to non-leaders. For example, these theories focus on traits such as intelligence or personality traits. Interest in leadership characteristics continues until today. In the 1940s and early 1950s, there was a shift in the literature which defined leadership as a behaviour in terms of directing group activities (Hemphill, 1949). Overall, **behavioural theories** examine what a leader does on the job rather than his or her traits. These studies focused on leader roles and responsibilities and identified effective behaviours related to leadership effectiveness. Researchers then began investigating which contextual and situational variables impact the effectiveness of leadership behaviours. The central idea driving **contingency theories** is that leaders can analyse their situations and tailor their behaviour to improve leadership effectiveness. The major situational variables include the characteristics of followers, characteristics of the work environment, follower tasks, and the external environment. Contingency theories, sometimes called **situational theories**, stress the importance of understanding leadership within a context rather than investigating leadership in a vacuum that is separate from aspects of the group and organisational environment. For example, leading in a small organisation in South Africa will be different from leading in a State-Owned Enterprises (SOE) in Tanzania. Later on, **influence theories**, which focus on the influence processes between leaders and followers, became popular. These studies examine the role of **charismatic leadership**, which refers to leadership influence based on the charismatic personality of the leader rather than position or formal authority. Since the late 1970s, researchers have focused on how leaders and followers interact and influence each other. **Relational theories** stress the relational processes that involve all the participants and further encourage individuals to contribute to achieving their vision. Some topics included under the umbrella of relational theories are servant leadership and team leadership. Finally, **implicit leadership theories** are personal assumptions about the traits and abilities that characterise an ideal organisational leader. These assumptions develop through socialisation and past experiences with leaders.

Leadership roles

To better understand leadership, it is important to examine the various roles performed by leaders. Based on the context, leaders are expected to engage in a set of activities or behaviours related to one's job. Leadership roles, a subset of the managerial roles that have been studied by Henry Mintzberg (1973) and other researchers, can provide some guidance in better comprehending the central ten roles of leadership.

Figurehead

Leaders spend some of their time as a figurehead, performing social, ceremonial, and legal responsibilities. The figurehead represents the organisation, as well as motivates the team to achieve goals. For people, this managerial role is a source of power and authority. Examples include attending a social event where they promote their company and greeting a potential business client and giving a tour. In the African context, leadership is a group phenomenon during which leaders support their followers and contribute to improving the life of the group, community, tribe, or village. Followers will honour and respect leaders in the formal hierarchical structures of chiefs and kings.

Spokesperson

Leaders spend their time being a spokesperson for their organisation and defending the company's interests. It is the leaders' responsibility to make the organisation look good in front of the stakeholders. Examples include attending the annual shareholders' meeting and speaking on behalf of the company at a conference.

Negotiator

Leaders participate in negotiations to attain their goals and may include negotiating with external parties, where they represent the interests of their organisations. They may also negotiate with internal parties, such as other departments or team members. Leaders who are more skilled at negotiating will more likely come to an agreement with customers, better organise the work process, and gain access to more resources. Examples include negotiating pricing, delivery, and design with customers, and negotiating access to capital and access to human capital (personnel) with seniors.

Coach and motivator

Leaders make the effort to coach and motivate their team members and inspire larger groups of people in their organisation. Examples include implementing rewards to encourage and motivate teams and inspiring staff by being charismatic and creating a vision.

Team builder

Leaders build effective teams. Examples include recognising team members for their accomplishments and encouraging team members by increasing team morale.

Team player

Leaders also need to be a good team player. Examples include cooperating with other organisations and departments and showing loyalty to superiors by supporting their plans.

Technical problem solver

Leaders need to assist solving technical problems, when needed. Examples include being a technical expert or adviser and making good decisions to help the company and performing tasks regularly, such as making sale calls.

Entrepreneur

Leaders need to be innovative and expand their organisations further. While leaders may not be self-employed, it's essential that they are intrapreneurial. Intrapreneurs are individuals who are tasked with creating new and innovative products within an already-established business. Examples include speaking with customers in order to be aware of changing needs, exploring opportunities, and developing new products and services.

Strategy developer

Executives and senior leaders need to develop the strategy of their organisation in collaboration with other members. Hence, they are able to shape the future of the organisation. Examples include setting a vision for the organisation and working on organisational policies.

Executor

Leaders must make a difference and implement strategies. Examples include placing accountability on others and converting strategies into action plans.

A common theme for these leadership roles is that the managerial leader inspires and influences others in some way. *Every* leader can make an important contribution to their organisation, whether it's being strategy developer or team player. This leads us to our next question: whether leadership is learned or acquired.

Are leaders born or made?

Largely a philosophical question, the answer to this question is both frustrating and expected. It's both. Research has shown that there is a genetic component to leadership. In other words, we have a genetic predisposition to human behaviour. In a 2007 study of female twins, it was concluded that "32% of the variance in leadership role occupancy was associated with heritability" (Arvey, Zhang, Avolio & Krueger, 2007). While there is a genetic component, the researchers concluded that prior life events and work experience also have an impact on leadership.

In essence, leaders are both born and made, as certain traits, motives, and characteristics are essential for leadership effectiveness. These attributes are impacted by a combination of heredity and the environment. For example, while there is predisposition to cognitive intelligence, when people have the right opportunities, they are able to develop their cognitive intelligence and be selected for a leadership position. Similarly, in the scenario in the beginning of the chapter, Okolloh is described as having "strong opinions" and "committed to helping others share their voices". These traits along with earning a Juris Doctor (the equivalent of a master's degree) from Harvard Law School and working as Google's Policy and Strategy Manager for Africa have impacted her leadership effectiveness (Leading Ladies Africa, 2022).

The art of followership

Even leaders may sometimes be followers in certain situations. For any organisation to succeed, there must be individuals who are willing to be effective followers, just as there must be those who are willing to lead (Sronce & Arendt, 2009). A **follower** is an individual who voluntarily accepts a leader's goals and influences and actively participates in pursuing goals. While our opening vignette focused on Ory Okolloh, the founder and leader who launched Ushahidi, Angela Oduor Lungati, current Chief Executive Officer, has followers with unique backgrounds and skillsets to empower the users to make their communities better, such as Director of Implementation, Chief Technology Officer, and Chief Operating Officer (Ushahidi, 2023).

Leadership and followership are fundamental roles that individuals shift into and out of depending on the situation. Despite the predominant focus on leadership, most of us often find ourselves in follower roles rather than leadership roles (Bennis, 2010). Hence, it is important for people to learn to manage both up and down in an organisational hierarchy. **Managing up** is a skill that helps people consciously and deliberately develop a highly effective relationship with their direct supervisor to obtain the best possible outcome for themselves, their boss, colleagues, and the organisation (Abbajay, 2018).

A framework for understanding leadership

Over time, we see that there have been many approaches to better understand leadership effectiveness. Earlier theories, such as the Great Man theories and Traits theories, largely focused on the traits associated with leadership effectiveness. Later on, the Situational and Contingency theories of leadership focused on the work environment, follower tasks, and the external environment. There have been several attempts to integrate

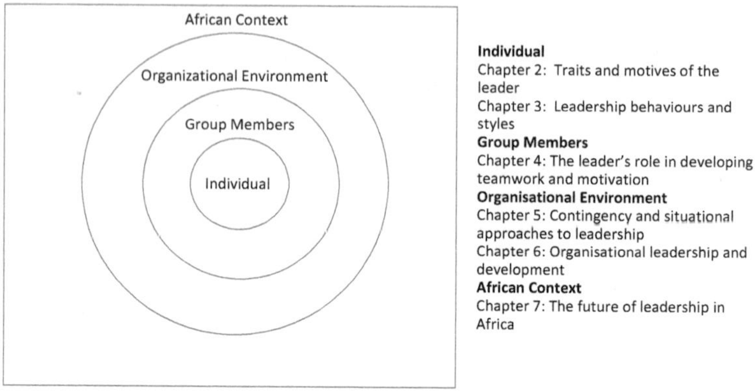

Figure 1.1 Framework for understanding leadership.

the various leadership theories in one framework. Kurt Lewin, considered the father of social psychology, first presented an equation that links the person and the environment: $B = f(P, E)$, where (1) B is behaviour; (2) P is person; and (3) E is the environment. Lewin believed in the importance of both the person and the environment in explaining individual's behaviour (Lewin, 1936). In line with Lewin's approach, we present the framework for understanding leadership in this book. Refer to Figure 1.1.

The framework presented emphasises the role of the African context in better understanding leadership effectiveness. According to our model, leadership in Africa can be understood by focusing on the leader's skills, motives, and behaviours; the leader's role in developing teamwork and team leadership; and the organisational context. It is important to understand that leadership does not occur in the vacuum. We now turn to the African context and examine the African continent from geographic, historical, economic, and cultural perspectives.

African context

According to a special report by the *Economist*, Africa is changing so rapidly; it is becoming hard to ignore. Jonathan Rosenthal, African editor of the *Economist*, noted that "Rapid economic and social change will give the continent a bigger role in world affairs" (Economist, 2020). Nevertheless, the African continent still needs to bounce back from the economic turnaround after the COVID-19 pandemic disruption. In addition, corruption continues to plague the continent (Transparency International, 2019). The majority of Africans (58%) say that corruption has increased. More specifically, 83% of South Africans surveyed stated that they have observed an increase in corruption. According to

José Ugaz, Chair of Transparency International, "Corruption creates and increases poverty and exclusion. While corrupt individuals with political power enjoy a lavish life, millions of Africans are deprived of their basic needs like food, health, education, housing, access to clean water and sanitation".

Despite these factors, Africa has much potential, and there are several opportunities for Africa in the future. Five trends that will create a new and improved way of doing business and provide opportunities that help growth in Africa are as follows (ALN, 2023):

1 E-Commerce Growth Persists Post-Pandemic: According to Statista, African online retail has been growing in recent years, and this trend is likely to continue. African countries, namely Nigeria, South Africa, Kenya, Morocco, and Egypt, have a thriving e-commerce market, including companies such as Jumia, Konga, Takealot, and Kilimall. Factors contributing to the growth are: access to reliable internet, availability of certain products, digital payment systems, and alternative payment methods. Furthermore, since Africa has the youngest population in the world, this sector has experienced significant growth.
2 Internet Connectivity to Vastly Improve Data Collection and Artificial Intelligence (AI) Capabilities: The internet has contributed to the expansion of many industries across Africa. In addition, access to information and data collection have been contributing factors to building businesses and learning the global trends in different industries. Several leading tech companies, such as Microsoft, Google, and Meta (Facebook), and various African tech companies, such as Flutterwave, are involved in Africa's digital transformation.
3 Businesses to Expand Communities and Commerce on Social Media: Social media and digital channels are currently underutilised in Africa; hence, many companies are interested to enhance their digital footprint. As the digital transformation continues to flourish, social media remains a key in growing audiences, clients, and potential customers and connecting the clients to brands. Moreover, digital channels have increased consumerism in many African economies, which has strengthened these economies.
4 Companies Focus on Sustainability: Due to climate change, governments and businesses are finding ways to incorporate sustainable business practices. According to a McKinsey Global Survey, 83% of C-suite leaders and investment specialists are confident that environmental, social, and corporate governance (ESG) programs will generate more shareholder value in the next five years (Kuyoro, Leke, White, Woetzel, & Jayaram, 2023). Several investors must incorporate ESG metrics (e.g., a company's carbon footprint, board diversity,

community development efforts, and water usage) in their investment decisions. Similarly, organisations must stress the importance of sustainability and avoid business practices that hurt the environment.

5 Adoption of Disruptive Technology: The term "disruptive" is used to describe a product that begins at the bottom of a market and continues to move up this market, eventually displacing or even replacing more established competing businesses. Several technologies in Africa have been able to cater certain aspects of services that are being overlooked. Hence, disruptive technologies and innovations have led to innovation-driven growth in Africa.

Below, we discuss the African continent from geographic, historical, economic, and cultural perspectives.

Geographic environment

According to the United Nations, there are 54 countries in Africa today (Worldmeters, 2023). Africa is the second largest continent of the world with over 11.5 million square miles. Africa is divided into regions – north, south, west, east, central, and Sub-Saharan (countries south of the Saharan desert, distinguished from the rest of Africa). African countries differ greatly regarding their size. On the one hand, the five top largest African countries include (1) Algeria which covers 6% of the Earth's total surface area—it is the largest country in Africa, and the tenth largest in the world; (2) The Democratic Republic of the Congo which is a landlocked country in Central Africa, larger than the combined land area of Norway, Sweden, Germany, France, and Spain; (3) Sudan situated in North Africa, sharing a coastal border with the Red Sea; (4) Libya, also situated in North Africa, sharing a coastal border with the Mediterranean Sea; and (5) Chad, a landlocked country in North-Central Africa.

On the other hand, the five top smallest countries in Africa by land area are all island nations: (1) Seychelles: an archipelago of 115 islands in the Indian Ocean; (2) São Tomé and Príncipe, two main islands of the archipelago located in the Gulf of Guinea; (3) Mauritius, located in the Indian Ocean, includes the Mascarene Islands of Rodrigues; (4) Comoros, archipelago of three main islands and numerous smaller islands, located in the Indian Ocean; and (5) Cape Verde, archipelago of ten islands, located in the Atlantic Ocean. The smallest country in mainland Africa is the Republic of Gambia and is almost completely surrounded by Senegal except for its western coastline along the Atlantic Ocean.

Historical environment

In addition to the geographical environment, it is important to understand the historical context. The historical context enables us to better understand the current leadership philosophies and practices in leadership. African history can be divided into eight separate time periods (Saylor Foundation, 2012).

Evolution

Africa is known as the "cradle of mankind". Hence, this period begins approximately 10 to 5 million B.C. when hominids evolved in Africa and moved out of the tropical rainforests to populate other parts of the continent. The evolution time period ends with the full development of *Homo sapiens* in roughly 40,000 B.C.

Pre-history

This period occurred before any written records and oral traditions from the past. During this time, we witnessed the full development of *Homo sapiens*. The prehistoric period ended with the development of written or oral records in specific localities. Interestingly, we see the important role of oral traditions and verbal communication as an important skill in leadership in Africa today. The prehistoric period is characterised by the formation of hunter-gatherer societies, pastoral societies, farming societies, and the advent of chieftaincies in Africa. While chieftaincies were developed in the pre-historic time period, we see the importance of chiefs even today in Africa. For example, Tieleman and Uitermark (2019) found that chieftaincies not only continue in the Ghanaian countryside but also play a role in new neighbourhoods on the outskirts of Ghana's fast-growing cities.

African state formation

During this period, many African states developed. Long-distance trade between the states became the foundation for the development. Early African states included: Mali, Songhay, Ghana, and the Swahili city-states. This time period was also characterised by elements of specialisation and hierarchy in African societies (Saylor Foundation, 2012).

Encounters with Europeans

During 1450–1815, African societies were greatly changed due to communication with the outside world. For example, trade between the African states and China developed. Also, new trading relationships were centred on slavery. The Atlantic slave trade largely characterised this time period. Approximately 11–15 million African slaves were taken from their communities and sent to the New World.

19th-Century legitimate commerce

During this period, the slave trade came to an end which was substituted with trade in legitimate goods, such as gold, palm oil, beeswax, gum arabic, rubber, ivory, gloves, and groundnuts. As a result, these goods became the new foundation for African trade with European merchants. Africa provided the resources for Europe's industrialisation and luxury items for Europe's upper and middle classes. Consequently, the legiti mate business impacted African societies with respect to power relationships and economic development.

Colonial period

During 1884 to the 1960s, most of Africa was under foreign domination. In 1884, European powers met at the Berlin Conference where the African continent was partitioned. The entire continent, with the exception of Ethiopia and Liberia, was colonised and exploited for the benefit of Europe. European colonialism lumped together peoples of diverse cultures and traditions, sometimes leading to secessionist movements and civil wars (Griffiths, 1986). These inherited boundaries continue to create problems for nation-building (Coplin, 1971). Africans were required to learn European languages, and there were special policies and cultural programs of assimilation. Even today, people may say "*yule jamaa ana roho ya kizungu*", translated to "the fellow has a white man's attitude", suggesting a better or superior approach, such as having good management skills (Melyoki & Punnett, 2021).

Decolonisation

Beginning in 1957 and lasting until 1975, African states became independent. Ghana first obtained its independence as the first sub-Saharan African state in 1957. By 1975, Mozambique and Angola became the last Portuguese colonies to gain their independence. This period was characterised by firm resistance and political activism on the part of African elites and ordinary citizens. The ideal of self-determination, as endorsed in the Charter of the United Nations, became reality for Africans.

Post-colonial period

This final period of African history began from the 1960s and the end of colonialism to today. After achieving independence, newly created African states were faced with the demands for political stability and socio-economic development. Historians, such as Catherine Coquery-Vidrovitch and Joseph K. Adjaye, continue to examine this period's achievements and failures. Refer to Manning and Miller (2019) for more information on historical writing in postcolonial Africa.

Economic environment

Overall, the economy of most of Africa can be characterised as underdeveloped, with the exception of South Africa and the countries of North Africa, which have diversified production systems (Britannica, 2023). The continent of Africa has abundant natural resources, but much of its economy has remained predominantly agricultural, and subsistence farming still engages more than 60% of the population (Britannica, 2023).

Economic growth in Sub-Saharan Africa (SSA) slowed down from 4.1% in 2021 to 3.6% in 2022. The decreased economic activity was largely due to the sluggish global economy, reduced (yet high) inflation rates, and difficult global and domestic financial conditions with high levels of debt (The World Bank, 2023). On the positive side, growth is estimated to increase to 3.7% and 3.9% in 2024 and 2025, respectively. Nevertheless, growth conditions are not enough to reduce extreme poverty and improve shared prosperity in the medium to long term. There is expected to be a reduction in recovery of per capita income growth in 2024 (at 1.2%) and the following year (at 1.4%) in 2025; nevertheless, it still has not yet reduced the region's poverty at pre-pandemic levels.

Despite reduced growth in Africa, a report by McKinsey Global Institute on *Reimagining economic growth in Africa: Turning diversity into opportunity* argues that the continent is home to the world's youngest and fastest-growing population, growing cities, and innovations in products ranging from fintech to clean energy (Kuyoro et al., 2023). With its population expected to nearly double to 2.5 billion people by 2050, the continent has a range of opportunities for strong growth that can develop its rich natural resources and human potential to increase wealth not only in Africa but around the world. We now turn to Africa's cultural environment.

Cultural environment

There are several frameworks, which examine cultural values in Africa, including The Leadership and Organisational Behavior Effectiveness (GLOBE) project (Wanasika, Howell, Litrell, & Dorfman, 2011) and Hofstede (1991). We use Hofstede's framework, one of the well-known models, which examine cultural values in several African countries. Hofstede defines culture as the mental programming of a given society to identify some of the values that could shape the behaviour of (African) employees. According to Hofstede, cultural values are classified along six dimensions: individualism/collectivism, power distance, femininity/masculinity, uncertainty avoidance, Confucian dynamism, and indulgence. Table 1.3 provides the data for Hofstede's cultural values for the available African countries. Overall, one can see that while Africans share certain cultural values, African countries also differ with respect to their scores.

Individualism/collectivism

Collectivism refers to the degree to which a given culture emphasises communal solidarity and the importance of a group. In general, most African countries expect each member to be loyal to the community, and members protect its interests. African countries typically rank high on collectivism given that extended family is the norm.

Power distance

Power distance refers to the degree to which differences in power are considered right and acceptable. In addition, this dimension refers to

Table 1.3 Hofstede's cultural values for African countries

Country	*Power Distance*	*Individualism*	*Masculinity*	*Uncertainty Avoidance*	*Confucian Dynamism*	*Indulgence*
Algeria	80	35	35	70	26	32
Angola	83	18	20	60	15	83
Burkino Faso	70	15	50	55	27	18
Cape Verde	75	20	15	40	12	83
Egypt	80	37	55	55	42	0
Ethiopia	70	20	65	55	—	46
Ghana	80	15	40	65	4	72
Kenya	70	25	60	50	—	—
Libya	100	35	66	67	15	74
Malawi	70	30	40	50	—	—
Morocco	70	46	53	68	14	25
Mozambique	85	15	38	44	11	80
Namibia	65	30	40	45	35	—
Nigeria	80	30	60	55	13	84
Senegal	70	25	45	55	25	—
Sierra Leone	70	20	40	50	—	—
South Africa	49	65	63	49	34	63
Tanzania	70	25	40	50	34	38
Tunisia	70	40	40	75	—	—
Zambia	60	35	40	50	30	42

Source: Based on Hofstede Insights (2023).

Notes: Boxes with "—" indicate that there is no score available for the country.

obedience to those in power. In general, African countries rank high on power distance and African employees defer to authority.

Masculinity/femininity

Masculinity refers to the degree to which traditional masculine values (e.g., assertiveness, achievement, material possessions) are more important than feminine values (e.g., nurturing and quality of life). The construct of masculinity also refers to the degree to which a culture favours traditional gender roles. That is, a highly feminine culture will see little differences between gender roles. In general, African cultures have a high differentiation with respect to gender roles.

Uncertainty avoidance

Uncertainty avoidance refers to the degree to which certainty is preferred over uncertainty and risk. Cultures high on uncertainty often emphasize maintaining traditions and the status quo compared to those cultures scoring low on this dimension. In general, African cultures typically rank high on uncertainty avoidance because traditions and customs are still important in most African countries.

Confucian dynamism

Confucian dynamism refers to the degree to which a society takes a long-term view and focuses on the future. Cultures that score high on Confucian dynamism plan for the future and value persistence and tradition. On the other hand, cultures that score low on this dimension value the present and accept change more rapidly. With respect to this dimension, one can see that there is more variance among African cultures. For example, Tanzania and South Africa scored 34 on this dimension compared to Ghana which scored 4.

Indulgence

Indulgence, relatively a new dimension to the model, refers to the degree to which people try to control their desires and impulses, based on the way they were raised. Cultures that score high on indulgence focus on gratification and enjoyment. On the other hand, cultures scoring low on this dimension prefer restraint, regulation, and try to control their impulses. Similar to Confucian dynamism, there is also variation among African countries on this dimension. For example, Cape Verde scored 83 on this dimension compared to Egypt which scored 0.

Leadership in Africa

Cultural frameworks, such as Hofstede (1991), contribute to our understanding of leadership in Africa. Generally, the literature examines the role of African values and systems to better understand leadership in the African context. One can categorise the literature into two general categories: studies focusing on (1) the application of Western theories to the African context and (2) Indigenous African leadership (Fourie, Van der Merwe, & Van der Merwe, 2015).

The first set of studies largely investigates the applicability of Western theory to the African contexts. For example, a cross-cultural study on transformational leadership, a Western developed construct, in Kenya and the U.S. findings suggest that transformational leadership was positively related to organisational commitment and job satisfaction in both cultures (Walumbwa, Orwa, & Wang, 2005). In addition, the Leadership and Organisational Behaviour Effectiveness (GLOBE) project, an integrated project of culture and leadership, also uncovered that some dimensions of leadership were more likely to successfully translate to Sub-Saharan Africa (SSA) compared to others (Wanasika et al., 2011). That is, Charismatic/Value-based and team-oriented leadership were seen as characteristics of outstanding leadership. Although Participation and Humane leadership were also endorsed, Autonomous and Self-Protective leadership were viewed as hindrances to outstanding leadership.

Unfortunately, management studies that test Western-based management theories in Africa do not sufficiently incorporate local issues and cultural factors that are central to the context (Galperin & Alamuri, 2017). Researchers recognise the limitations of transferring Western constructs to the African context and stress the need for incorporating the local contextual factors (Beaugré & Offodile, 2001; Bewaji, 2003).

The second category examines Indigenous theories that emerged from the African context. According to Murithi (2008), Indigenous is defined as that which is inherent from within a given society and therefore has become innate or instinctive to it. Given the constraints of Western theories in understanding African leadership, indigenised models of leadership provide a more culturally oriented models of leadership. For example, researchers examine *Ubuntu* as a leadership philosophy. As noted earlier, *Ubuntu* emphasises collectivism and relationships over material objects and includes opportunities, responsibilities, and challenges. When applying *Ubuntu* in an organisational context, Malunga (2009) stresses leadership and decision-making as participatory, transparent, and democratic. Researchers also believe that the concept of *Ubuntu* in an organisational context must stress African collective solidarity, community networks, and social sensitivity in the development of leadership and management practices (Iwowo, 2015).

There have also been efforts to examine leadership in Africa from a "blank slate" perspective. The Leadership Effectiveness in Africa and the Diaspora (LEAD) Project began with emic, or culture-specific, research and used results from this approach to develop an etic large-scale survey to examine leadership effectiveness in Africa (Lituchy, Galperin, & Punnett, 2017). The LEAD Scale is a culturally sensitive measure of leadership effectiveness in Africa and the African diaspora (Michaud et al., 2020).

Conclusion

By providing a contextual background and discussing the African continent from geographic, historical, economic, and cultural perspectives, we can better understand leadership in Africa. When examining leadership in Africa, it is essential to take a decolonised view and focus on the role of cultural values and their impact on leadership. Furthermore, it is important to consider the role of the organisational culture. By taking note of these contextual factors, managers will be able to lead more effectively in Africa.

Discussion questions

- What are the challenges and opportunities that managers may face when leading in Africa?
- How has COVID-19 impacted leadership in Africa?
- How does leadership differ from management?
- Describe the main leadership approaches in the literature and their transferability to Africa?
- Are leaders born or made?
- In your opinion, what trends will impact Africa in the next five years? Ten years?

Exercise 1:What is leadership to you?

There exist many definitions of leadership in the literature. As shown in Table 1.1, some of the world's top CEOs shared their definition of leadership. We want to know: What is leadership to you? Select a definition of leadership that best fits you. If you do not see a definition that fits you, feel free to share your own definition. How have your personal values and cultural values impacted your selection and/or definition of leadership? Write a 500-word essay.

References

Abbajay, M. (2018). *Managing up: How to move up, win at work, and succeed with any type of boss*. Hoboken, NJ: John Wiley & Sons.

African Leadership Institute (2018). An abundance of young African leaders but no seats at the table. https://alinstitute.org/images/downloads/AFLILeadershipReport2018.pdf

ALN (2023). Trends and Opportunities for Businesses in Africa in 2023. Retrieved from https://aln.africa/news/trends-and-opportunities-for-businesses-in-africa-in-2023/

Arvey, R. D., Zhang, Z., Avolio, B. J., & Krueger, R. F. (2007). Developmental and genetic determinants of leadership role occupancy among women. *Journal of Applied Psychology*, *92*(3), 693–706. https://doi.org/10.1037/0021-9010.92.3.693

Beaugré, C. D., & Offodile, O. F. (2001). Managing for organizational effectiveness in sub-Saharan Africa: a culture-fit model. *International Journal of Human Resource Management*, *12*, 535–550.

Bennis, W. (2010). Art of followership: Followers engage in an interdependent dance. *Leadership Excellence*, *27*, 3–4.

Bewaji, J. A. I. (2003). Leadership – A philosophical exploration of perspectives in African, Caribbean and Diaspora polities. *Journal on African Philosophy*, 2, 1–43.

Britannica (2023). Economy of Africa. Retrieved from https://www.britannica.com/place/Africa/Economy

Coplin, D. W. (1971). *Introduction to international politics. A Theoretical Overview*. Chicago, IL: Markham publishing Co.

Eades, J. (2023). What happens to a leaderless team? Retrieved from https://learnloft.com/2016/04/12/what-happens-to-a-leaderless-team/#:~:text=Without%20good%20communication%2C%20teams%20become,the%20team%20members%20step%20up.

Eckert, R., & Rweyongoza, S. (2020). Leadership development in Africa a focus on strengths. *Center for Creative Leadership*. Retrieved from https://cclinnovation.org/wp-content/uploads/2020/02/leadershipdevelopmentafrica.pdf

Economist (2020). Africa is changing so rapidly, it is becoming hard to ignore. *The Economist*, Special Report. March 28, 2020. https://www.economist.com/special-report/2020/03/26/africa-is-changing-so-rapidly-it-is-becoming-hard-to-ignore

Fourie, W., Van der Merwe, S., & Van der Merwe, B. (2015). Sixty years of research on leadership in Africa: A review of the literature. *Leadership*, *13*(2), 222–251. https://doi.org/10.1177/1742715015580665

Galperin, B. L., & Alamuri, S. (2017). Leadership styles and quality in Africa: A literature review. In T. R. Lituchy, B. L. Galperin, & B. J. Punnett (Eds.), *LEAD: Leadership effectiveness in Africa and the African Diaspora* (pp. 33–44). New York, NY: Palgrave McMillan.

Griffiths, I. (1986). The scramble for Africa: Inherited political boundaries. *The Geographical Journal*, *152*, 204–216.

Goodreads (2003). Quotes. Retrieved from https://www.goodreads.com/quotes/7408405-seth-godin-writes-leadership-is-scarce-because-few-people-are

Hemphill, J. K. (1949). *Situational factors in leadership*. Columbus Ohio State University: Bureau of Educational Research.

Hofstede, G. (1991). *Culture and organization. Software of the mind*. London, England: McGraw-Hill.

Hofstede Insights (2023). Country comparison tool. Retrieved from https://www.hofstede-insights.com/country-comparison-tool

Iwowo, V. (2015). Leadership in Africa: Rethinking development. *Personnel Review*, *44*, 408–429. http://doi.org/10.1108/PR-07-2013-0128

Kim, W. K., & Maubourgne, R. A. (1992). Parables of Leadership. *Harvard Business Review*, July-August, 123.

Kuyoro, M., Leke, A., White, O., Woetzel, L., & Jayaram, K. (2023). Reimagining economic growth in Africa: Turning diversity into opportunity. *McKinsey Global Institute*. Retrieved from https://www.mckinsey.com/mgi/our-research/reimagining-economic-growth-in-africa-turning-diversity-into-opportunity

Leading Ladies Africa (2022). #LeadingLadySpotlight: Ory Okolloh, Kenyan activist and Founder, Ushahidi. Retrieved January 19, 2022, from https://leadingladiesafrica.org/leadingladyspotlight-ory-okolloh-kenyan-activist-and-founder-ushahidi/

Lewin, K. (1936). *Principles of topological psychology* (pp. 12). New York, NY: McGraw-Hill.

Lituchy, T. R., Galperin, B. L., & Punnett, B. J. (2017). *LEAD: Leadership effectiveness in Africa and the African Diaspora*. New York, NY: Palgrave McMillan.

Malunga, C. (2009). *Understanding organizational leadership through Ubuntu*. Aso, Nigeria: Adonis & Abbey Publishers Ltd.

Manning, P., & Miller, J. (2019). Historical writing in postcolonial Africa: The institutional context. *The International Journal of African Historical Studies*, *52*(2), 191–216.

Melyoki, L. L., & Punnett, B. J. (2021). *Essentials of general management in Africa*. Taylor & Francis: NY.

Meier, P., & Brodock, K. (2008). Crisis mapping Kenya's election violence: Comparing mainstream news. In *Citizen journalism and Ushahidi*. Boston, MA: Harvard Humanitarian Initiative, Harvard University. https://irevolutions.org/2008/10/23/mapping-kenyas-election-violence/

Michaud, J., Lvina, E., Galperin, B. L., Lituchy, T. R., Punnett, B. J., Taleb, A., … Alleyne, A. (2020). Development and validation of the Leadership Effectiveness in Africa and the Diaspora (LEAD) scale. *International Journal of Cross Cultural Management*, *20*(3), 361–384. https://doi.org/10.1177/1470595820973438

Mintzberg, H. (1973). *The nature of managerial work*. New York, NY: Harper and Row.

Mintzberg, H. (2009). *Managing*. San Francisco, CA: Berrett-Koehler Publishers.

Mulupi, D. (2012). Meet the boss: James Mworia, CEO, Centum. *How We Made Africa*. Retrieved February 23, 2024, from https://www.howwemadeitinafrica.com/meet-the-boss-james-mworia-ceo-centum/18606/

Moore, B. V. (1927). The May conference on leadership. *Personnel Journal*, *6*, 124–128.

Morgan, J. (2020). 14 top CEOs share their definition of "leadership," what's yours?. Retrieved August 13, 2020, from https://medium.com/jacob-morgan/14-top-ceos-share-their-definition-of-leadership-whats-yours-2b89a58576a6

Murithi, T. (2008). African indigenous and endogenous approaches to peace and conflict resolution. In D. J. Francis (Ed.), *Peace and conflict in Africa* (pp. 288). Zed Books Ltd. ISBN-13: 978-1842779545

Oberholster, T. (2023). Leadership in uncertain times. *Acumen*, *45*, 10–13.

O'Leary, J. (2016). Do managers and leaders really do different things? *Harvard Business Review*, *June*(20), 1–5. https://hbr.org/2016/06/do-managers-and-leaders-really-do-different-things

Saylor Foundation (2012). Major periods in African history. Retrieved from https://resources.saylor.org/wwwresources/archived/site/wp-content/uploads/2012/05/hist252-1.2-Major-Periods-in-African-History.pdf

Sronce, R., & Arendt, L. A. (2009). Demonstrating the interplay of leaders and followers. *Journal of Management Education*, *33*, 699–724.

Stogdill, R. M. (1974). *Handbook of leadership: A survey of theory and research*. New York, NY: Free Press.

The World Bank (2023). The World Bank in Africa. Retrieved from https://www.worldbank.org/en/region/afr/overview

Tieleman, J., & Uitermark, J. (2019). Chiefs in the city: Traditional authority in the modern state. *Sociology*, *53*(4), 707–723. https://doi.org/10.1177/0038038518809325

Transparency International (2019). Corruption in Africa: 75 million people pay bribes. https://www.transparency.org/en/gcb/africa/africa-9th-edition

Ugwuegbu, D. C. E. (2001). *The psychology of management in African Organizations*. Westport, CT: Quorum Books: Greenwood.

Ushahidi (2023). A global team, advancing technology and social change. Our team. Retrieved from https://www.ushahidi.com/about/team/

Walumbwa, F. O., Orwa, B., & Wang, P. (2005). Transformational leadership, organizational commitment, and job satisfaction: A comparative study of Kenyan and U.S. financial firms. *Human Resources Development Quarterly*, *16*, 235–256.

Wanasika, I., Howell, J. P. Litrell, R., & Dorfman, P. (2011). Managerial leadership and culture in Sub-Saharan Africa. *Journal of World Business*, *46*, 234–241.

Worldmeters (2023). Countries in Africa. Retrieved from https://www.worldometers.info/geography/how-many-countries-in-africa/

2 Traits and motives of the leader

Chapter summary

This chapter identifies the general and task-related traits and discusses the cognitive factors that contribute to leadership effectiveness. The chapter also identifies the central motives related to leadership effectiveness. Finally, the chapter concludes by discussing the strengths and weaknesses of the trait approach to leadership and identifies the important attributes of leadership effectiveness in Africa.

Learning objectives

After studying this chapter, you should be able to do the following:

- Identify the general and task-related traits that contribute to leadership effectiveness.
- Identify the cognitive factors related to leadership effectiveness.
- Describe the key leadership motives related to leadership.
- Discuss the strengths and weaknesses of the trait approach.
- Identify the important attributes of leadership effectiveness in Africa.

Nelson Mandela was the first Black president of South Africa and was an instrumental figure in ending apartheid. Mandela gained recognition by fighting against the oppressive measures of the apartheid regime and for democracy in South Africa. He was imprisoned for 27 years and later vindicated. In 1993, Mandela was jointly awarded the Nobel Peace Prize with his former adversary, President F. W. de Klerk, South Africa's last apartheid leader (Freiberg & Freiberg, 2018). Nelson Mandela later became an advocate for social and human rights organisations. Given Mandela's legacy as an iconic leader in South Africa and the global

DOI: 10.4324/9781003020523-2

community, Mandela has been described as a "true leader" (Lowe, 2022) and has been recognised as having the leadership qualities that made him a successful leader. In a study analysing the depiction of Mandela's personality traits in poetry, Mandela's personality was described as possessing bravery, determination, humility, goodness, peace, and tactical skills (Mtumane & Bobelo, 2008).

Our chapter discusses the personality traits of effective leaders. This chapter identifies the general and task-related traits and discusses the cognitive factors that contribute to leadership effectiveness. For example, Mandela was described as a humble leader. Humility, a general personality trait, has been found to be related to effective leadership. The chapter also identifies the central motives related to leadership effectiveness. Finally, the chapter concludes by discussing the strengths and weaknesses of the trait approach to leadership and identifies the important attributes of leadership effectiveness in Africa.

The trait approach

By the 20th century, the **Great Man theories** developed into **trait theories** which focused on the traits of leaders—that is, people's general characteristics, including capacities, motives, or patterns of behaviour. According to trait theories, leaders' characteristics are different from non-leaders. Traits included both physical attributes, such as height, weight, and physique, which were heavily dependent on heredity, and other attributes based on experience and learning, such as knowledge of the industry (Kirkpatrick & Locke, 1991).

More recently, the trait-based approach to leadership has become more popular. Research has shown that a wide range of traits and characteristics influence leadership effectiveness and outcomes (Zaccaro, Green, Dubrow, & Koize, 2018).

In general, characteristics associated with leadership can be organised into three main categories: (1) personality traits, (2) motives, and (3) cognitive factors. It should be noted that these groupings are not strict categories but rather useful classifications.

Personality traits of effective leaders

Personality traits can be grouped into two main categories: general personality traits and task-related traits. Table 2.1 refers to both the general personality and task-related personality traits identified in the literature. While general personality traits are seen both within and outside the context of work and are related to the success and satisfaction in both work and personal life, task-related traits are closely related to task accomplishment.

Table 2.1 Personality traits

General personality traits	*Task-related personality traits*
Self-confidence	Proactive personality
Humility	Mindfulness
Core-self evaluations	Flexibility and adaptability
Trustworthiness	Courage
Authenticity	Emotional intelligence
Extraversion	
Assertiveness	
Enthusiasm, passion, optimism, warmth	
Sense of humour	
The Likability factor	

Source: Based on Dubrin (2023).

General personality traits

The leadership literature outlines several general personality traits that contribute to leadership effectiveness. In particular, African leaders excel in interpersonal skills and show their genuine interest in the well-being and relationships of their team members (Hogan Assessments, 2023). African leaders are also typically more humble and selfless compared to Western leaders who are more ambitious and competitive. The main general personality traits found in many situations are discussed below.

Self-confidence

Self-confidence is a feeling of trust in one's abilities, qualities, and judgment. Self-confidence, one of the first leadership traits examined in the literature, is still seen as an important contributor to leadership effectiveness. In general, self-confidence can improve performance in a broad range of tasks (DeRue, Nahrgang, Wellman, & Humphrey, 2011).

Humility

Humility is defined as self-awareness, appreciating the strengths and contributions of others, openness to ideas, and feedback regarding one's performance (Assessment Systems, 2023). When leaders display humility, they are better able to make educated decisions regarding task performance.

Core-self evaluations

Core-self evaluations, a general personality trait, represent a wide range of personality traits, including self-esteem, locus of control, self-efficacy, and emotional stability. Overall, leaders with positive self-evaluations are more likely to make decisions more quickly and execute decisions because they feel they are in control.

Trustworthiness

Trustworthiness, one of the foundations of leadership, is the ability to be relied on as honest or truthful (Frei & Morriss, 2020). Leaders must be trustworthy in the eyes of team members and also be able to trust their team. Since leaders play such a crucial role in shaping organisational culture and defining norms of behaviours, leaders must focus on establishing trust or risk a breakdown in communication, collaboration, and innovation.

Authenticity

Authenticity, related to trustworthiness, refers to being genuine and honest about your personality, values, and beliefs. Some characteristics of authentic leaders include a commitment to self-improvement, cultivation of self-awareness, discipline, a sense of mission, and the ability to inspire faith in others (Gavin, 2019).

Extraversion

Extraversion (also often spelled extroversion) is a personality trait or style characterised by a preference for or orientation to engaging socially with others and includes qualities such as talkative, energetic, assertive, and outgoing. Extraversion is one of the **Big Five Personality traits**, which are also classified as the five broad dimensions of personality first developed by D. W. Fiske in 1949. The other traits classified into these five dimensions include agreeableness, openness, conscientiousness, and neuroticism (Fiske, 1949).

Extraverts are more likely to take on leadership roles and participate in group activities. In a meta-analytic study of 11,705 participants, extraversion was the most consistent personality trait related to emergence or the perception of being a leader and being able to lead effectively (Judge, Bono, Ilies, & Gerhardt, 2002). Charismatic/value-based leadership was also identified as one of the six global leadership styles identified in the GLOBE project as mentioned in Chapter 1 (Wanasika, Howell, Litrell, & Dorfman, 2011). While extraverted leaders are often seen as more effective leaders, research by Adam Grant argues that introverted leaders can be more effective than extraverts in certain circumstances (Grant, 2010).

Assertiveness

Assertiveness, related to extraversion, refers to being straightforward in communicating demands, opinions, feelings, and attitudes. Leaders who are assertive are more likely to perform tasks and achieve goals. Assertive leaders are also more likely to demand results and establish higher performance expectations. While assertiveness is often related to strong leadership, some cultures which prioritise harmony and respect and the collective welfare may perceive individual assertiveness as aggressive and disrespectful. In line with the GLOBE project, the self-sacrificial and internally competitive leadership attributes are culturally contingent leadership traits which require some adaptation across cultural contexts (Wanasika et al., 2011).

Enthusiasm, passion, optimism, and warmth

Being a leader is more than just setting expectations and demanding results. Enthusiasm, passion, optimism, and warmth contribute to leadership effectiveness by creating opportunities and helping achieve goals.

Sense of humour

A sense of humour refers to the ability to find things funny, a general enjoyment in doing so, or the particular types of things one finds funny. Humour in leadership, a key element of organisational effectiveness and business success, has attracted an increased amount of empirical research (Cooper, Kong, & Crossley, 2018; Kong, Cooper, & Sosik, 2019).

The Likability factor

The Likability factor refers to whether a leader is liked by his/her group members. A key aspect of likability is whether a leader is friendly to others. Leaders who are easy to talk to, warm, and generally positive are seen as more likable to those that are not.

Task-related personality traits

Task-related personality traits are traits closely related to task accomplishment. These traits discussed in the following section.

Proactive personality

Proactive personality refers to a stable tendency to take personal initiative in a broad range of activities and situations (Seibert, Kraimer, &

Crant, 2001). People with proactive personalities seek out opportunities and act on them; show initiative and take action; and persevere until the meaningful desired change occurs. It follows that leaders are more likely to have proactive personalities.

Mindfulness

Mindfulness refers to "a state of non-judgmental attentiveness to and awareness of moment to moment experiences" (Hülsheger, Alberts, Feinholdt, & Lang, 2013). Leaders who practice mindfulness possess traits and behaviours associated with effective leadership, such as observance, perceptiveness, and attention to detail, which assist in gaining a better understanding of the bigger picture.

Flexibility and adaptability

Flexibility is the ability to adjust to different situations. Given the uncertain and complex world that we live in, adaptability is a requirement. Leaders must be flexible to succeed. According to the Center for Creative Leadership (2021), adaptability is about being able to behave in a variety of ways that enable leaders to shift and experiment as things change. While adaptability is an important attribute for all leaders, a recent survey suggests that adaptability is one of the top attributes African employers are looking for today (Odinaka, 2022).

Courage

Being courageous is a central component of strong leadership. Leaders who are courageous can acknowledge their ignorance and are able to own their mistakes with humility. Courageous leaders have the integrity that is necessary to have difficult conversations, even when they know it may make the other person feel bad. Finally, courageous leaders associate themselves with and promote people who help them learn by challenging rather than flattering them (Detert, 2022).

Emotional intelligence

Emotional intelligence (EI) refers to a person's abilities to perceive, identify, understand, and successfully manage emotions in themselves and others. EI can be learned and developed. Several studies have shown the importance of EI in leadership effectiveness. When leaders are emotionally intelligent, they are more likely to effectively manage themselves and their relationships (Goleman, 2000; Mayer, Caruso, & Salovey, 1999).

Leaders with higher levels of emotional intelligence received higher effectiveness ratings from both peers and subordinates (Bono & Ilies, 2006). Research has also shown that leaders with higher levels of emotional intelligence foster better work climates and have higher employee engagement (Korn Ferry, 2023).

There are four components of emotional intelligence: self-awareness, self-management, social awareness, and relationship management. Refer to Table 2.2 for the components of Emotional Intelligence.

Cognitive factors and leadership

In addition to general and task-related traits, cognitive factors, such as problem-solving and intellectual skills, also contribute to leadership effectiveness. Refer to Table 2.3 for a list of cognitive factors related to leadership. That is, mental abilities or the ability to organise information and then store the information in memory are important factors in leadership. Overall, research has shown that cognitive ability positively relates to leadership success, but this relationship is weaker in non-leadership roles and varies across different situations and criteria (Bergner, 2020).

Charisma

Finally, charisma is the quality of being able to attract, charm, and influence those around you; it is an important quality of leaders whose purposes, powers, and extraordinary determination differentiates charismatic leaders from others (Conger & Kanungo, 1998). That is, people who are charismatic have a charming and colourful personality. Charismatic leaders in Africa include Nelson Mandela, former president of South Africa, and Julius Nyerere, former president of Tanzania.

Charismatic leadership, an extension of trait theory, has become important to leadership effectiveness because charisma enables leaders to carry their roles. Charisma is a desirable quality that makes others want to be led by the person who possesses this quality. An important dimension of charisma is that charisma is based on perceptions, and charismatic leadership involves the attributions made by group members about the characteristics of leaders and the results they achieve.

One of the key characteristics of charismatic leaders is that they are able to attract, motivate, and lead others. Since charisma is one of the central characteristics of transformational leadership, charismatic leaders often create change. A **transformational leader** is one who brings about positive and major changes in an organisation. Nevertheless, it should be noted that many charismatic leaders are not transformational.

Table 2.2 Four components of emotional intelligence

Self		*Others*
Awareness (Who I am?)	*Self-awareness* • Emotional self-awareness: the ability to know oneself and understand one's feelings. • Accurate self-assessment: understanding one's strengths and weaknesses, and their effects. • Self-confidence: having faith in oneself and being willing to put oneself forward.	*Social-awareness* • Empathy: the ability to form connections with others, understanding, and acknowledging others' emotions. • Service orientation: being helpful, contributing to the group effort, and displaying good listening skills. • Organisational awareness: the ability to explain oneself well and be aware of how you are being understood, as well as sensing the level of comprehension of your audience.
Regulation (What I do?)	*Self-management* • Emotional self-control: an important part of emotional maturity, controlling one's feelings and/or expressing them in the appropriate settings is a key skill. • Achievement: being goal-oriented and being able to work towards one's goals. • Initiative: being self-motivated, and having the ability to keep working despite setbacks. • Transparency: being honest and open, interacting with integrity, and being trustworthy. • Adaptability: showing resilience and the ability to change course when necessary. • Optimism: having a positive outlook, hoping for the best and preparing for success.	*Relationship management* • Inspirational leadership: being a good mentor, role model, and authority figure. • Influence: articulating points in persuasive and clear ways that effectively motivate others. • Conflict management: having the skills to improve relationships, negotiate, and lead. The ability to settle disputes, differences of opinion, and misunderstandings. • Teamwork and collaboration: working with others in an effective manner.

Source: Adapted from Boyatzis and Goleman (2001).

Table 2.3 Cognitive factors and leadership

Cognitive (or analytical intelligence)
• An effective leader can figure out how to make appropriate use of **artificial intelligence (AI)** or the ability of a computer program or machine to think and learn in a manner that mirrors human intelligence.
• An effective leader will also make use of **practical intelligence** or the ability to solve everyday problems by using experience-based knowledge to adapt and shape the environment.
Knowledge of the business or group task
• An effective leader has to be technically competent in some areas, particularly when leading specialists.
• Leaders are expected to bring useful ideas to the group and organisation.
Creativity
• An effective leader will be creative in developing original solutions to complex problems.
Insight into people and situations
• An effective leader has **insight** or a depth of understanding that requires intuition and common sense.
• An effective leader has insight into people and situations in order to help him/her make best use of their own and others' talents.
Farsightedness and conceptual thinking
• An effective leader has **farsightedness** or the ability to understand the long-range implications of actions and policies.
• An effective leader has **conceptual thinking** or the ability to see the overall perspective, making farsightedness possible.

Source: Adapted from Dubrin (2023).

While charismatic leaders may inspire people, they may not bring about a change. In Chapter 3, we will expand on the transformational leadership style.

Leadership motives

Based on the above, one can see that leaders have a desire to occupy a position of responsibility for others. Effective leaders differ based on their motives and needs (Dubrin, 2023). The five different motives are as follows:

- **Motivation to lead** or the desire to attain leadership roles, as well as meet the requirements of a leadership role.
- **The power motive** or the strong need to control resources. Leaders with a power motive are interested in influencing others. Power can be used for the sake of the power holder (personalised power motive) or for helping others (socialised power motive).

- **Drive and achievement motive.** Drive refers to a propensity to put energy into achieving objectives and persistence in applying the energy. Drive also encompasses **achievement motivation** or finding joy in accomplishing tasks for their intrinsic value.
- **Tenacity and resilience. Tenacity** or grit refers to stamina needed to keep pushing forward when setbacks surface. Resilience is part of tenacity because a tenacious person will pull through despite setbacks. Since it may take a long time to close a deal or start a new program, tenacity and resilience are important motives for leadership.

Strengths and limitations of the trait approach

The trait approach has contributed to our understanding of leadership by outlining the key personal characteristics differentiating leaders from non-leaders. More recently, the trait approach has gained more popularity with the focus on emotional intelligence, charisma, innovative thinking, and ethical conduct. The trait approach can provide some insights into leadership selection. If we know that integrity and creativity are important leadership traits, we can focus on selecting leaders with those traits. Also, the trait approach can assist in preparing people for leadership responsibility by developing the key attributes, such as humility and a sense of humour. Despite the strengths of this approach, the trait theory does not indicate which traits are needed in which leadership situations. Furthermore, when adopting a trait approach perspective, some leaders may emphasise the importance of one trait (e.g., extraversion) while disregarding its polar oppositive (e.g., introversion). This perspective may decrease leadership effectiveness as a combination of opposites may be needed given the particular situation. Trait approach is based on research conducted in the West rather than emerging countries such as Africa. Finally, effective leadership does not only depend on the leader's traits but rather the appropriate leadership style given the leadership situation, context, and motives. We now turn to attributes of leadership effectiveness in Africa. For a complete discussion on the role of the situation, refer to Chapter 5 on contingency and situational approaches of leadership.

Attributes of leadership effectiveness in Africa

While research suggests the main characteristics of effective leaders across some Western cultures (Muchiri, 2011), debate remains about perceptions of effective leadership across cultures (Den Hartog, House, Hanges, Ruiz-Quintanilla, & Dorfman, 1999). According to the GLOBE project, universally endorsed attributes related to charismatic leadership included encouraging, positive, motivational, confidence builder, dynamic, and foresight. On the other hand, culturally contingent items related to charismatic leadership related to risk-taking, compassionate, enthusiastic, and sensitive. For example, what is considered risk-taking in one context may not be in another context. The literature also suggests that the *Ubuntu* philosophy, which focuses on African solidarity, community networks, and social sensitivity, promote selfless and empathetic leaders. Refer to Chapter 1 for a discussion on *Ubuntu*.

Similarly, the LEAD research project started with the aim to better understand perceptions of what constitutes effectiveness of leadership in Africa and the African diaspora (Lituchy, Galperin, & Punnett, 2017). Using the Delphi technique and focus groups, one of the questions that participants were asked was, "What three to five words/phrases would you use to describe an effective leader's personal characteristics?" Data were collected from African countries (Senaji et al., 2014), including Egypt, Ghana, Kenya, Nigeria, and Uganda ($N = 94$). The findings suggest that, first, being a visionary was the most important descriptor of effective leaders, followed by descriptors such as knowledge, intelligent, education, or well-educated. The third most important description was team leader/team player. Finally, charisma was also found to be an important attribute. The other descriptors of effective leaders included competence and good communication skills in Ghana; result-/solution-orientated and influence in Kenya; and humble and selfless in Nigeria.

The LEAD research project also investigated leadership motives. Another question asked about leadership motivation to succeed was, "What three to five words/phrases describe what motivates leaders to succeed?" Participants in all five countries agreed that involvement with people and society and having the support of one's subordinates were important motivators for leaders. Having a desire to succeed or a sense of self-fulfilment was a key motivator for leaders in Ghana, Kenya, Nigeria, and Uganda. Extrinsic motivators, including money and wealth, were considered important motivators for leaders to succeed by participants from Egypt, Kenya, Nigeria, and Uganda. Finally, seeking justice for others also motivated leaders to succeed. Dedication, desire to achieve targets/results, joy of success, cooperation from the people being led, and the need to serve were words/phrases used to describe what motivates leaders to succeed in Kenya. Participants in Nigeria and Uganda mentioned the community/society.

Conclusion

Overall, when examining the differences in attributes and motivations in Africa, one is able to see more of an emphasis on the community. In general, African leaders typically have a more holistic view of leadership than their Western counterparts. African leaders view leadership as a process that extends beyond the individual leader and includes the entire community. Hence, it becomes evident that perceptions of attributes of leadership effectiveness and leadership motivations in Africa tend to be more collectivistic, emphasising qualities such as being a team player (attribute) and being motivated to seek justice for others.

Discussion questions

- Based on the list of leadership attributes provided, which are the key general and task-related traits that contribute to leadership effectiveness in Africa? Explain why you think these are important.
- In your opinion, are there any additional leadership attributes not mentioned in this chapter which relate to leadership effectiveness in Africa?
- Given the changes in the technological context, how do you see AI impacting the nature of work and the specific traits that contribute to leadership effectiveness in Africa in the next five to seven years?
- There are five leadership motives listed in this chapter. What is your primary motivation to lead?

Exercise 1: Do you show flexible leadership? How well do you adapt to change?

As noted earlier, African employers are looking for adaptable employees. Consider your personal approach to change. How do you respond when adapting to change? Indicate your strength of agreement with each of the following statements: (1) strongly disagree (SD); (2) disagree (D); (3) neutral (N); (4) agree (A); and strongly agree (SA).

Table 2.4 Your personal approach to change?

		SD	*D*	*N*	*A*	*SA*
1	I accept change as positive.	1	2	3	4	5
2	I see change as an opportunity.	1	2	3	4	5
3	I adapt plans as necessary.	1	2	3	4	5
4	I quickly master new technology, vocabulary, operating rules.	1	2	3	4	5
5	I lead change by example.	1	2	3	4	5
6	I take into account other people's concerns.	1	2	3	4	5
7	I sort out my strengths and weaknesses fairly accurately.	1	2	3	4	5
8	I admit to my personal mistakes, learn from them, and move on.	1	2	3	4	5
9	I remain optimistic.	1	2	3	4	5

Source: Based on Center for Creative Leadership (2021).

Scoring and interpretation: Find your total score by summing the point values for each question.

39—45: You are probably adaptable, which should help you as a leader.
23—38: You are probably neutral, neither dislike nor embrace change.
9—22: You probably feel more uncomfortable with change.

If few or none of these responses describes you, you're not alone. Many of us get stuck, experience anxiety with change, have a hard time letting go, or simply don't know how to proceed in unknown territory. Some suggestions to increase your adaptability include seeking out new experiences and opportunities and practicing self-awareness to better understand how you react in various situations.

Exercise 2: Attributes and motives of great African leaders

Some of the great Africa leaders in history include Nelson Mandela, Haile Selassie, Kwame Nkrumah, Julius Nyerere, Patrice Lumumba, Jomo Kenyatta, Thomas Sankara, Nnamdi Azikiwe, Kofi Annan, and Ellen Johnson-Sirleaf. Discuss the leadership attributes of these leaders. What were their motives? Write a 500-word essay.

References

Assessment Systems (2023). The importance of humility in leadership (Interview with Dr. Robert Hogan). https://asystems.as/inspirations/the-importance-of-humility-in-leadership-interview-with-dr-robert-hogan/#:~:text=Humility%20is%20broadly%20defined%20as,informed%20decisions%20about%20task%20performance

Bergner, S. (2020). Being smart is not enough: Personality traits and vocational interests incrementally predict intention, status and success of leaders and entrepreneurs beyond cognitive ability. *Frontiers in Psychology*, *11*. https://doi.org/10.3389/fpsyg.2020.00204

Bono, J. E., & Ilies, R. (2006). Charisma, positive emotions and mood contagion. *The Leadership Quarterly*, *17*, 317–334. http://doi.org/10.1016/j.leaqua.2006.04.008

Boyatzis, R., & Goleman, D. (2001). *The emotional competence inventory (ECI)* (University Edition). Boston, MA: The Hay Group.

Center for Creative Leadership (2021). Adapting to change requires flexible leaders. Retrieved August 24, 2021, from https://www.ccl.org/articles/leading-effectively-articles/adaptability-1-idea-3-facts-5-tips/#:~:text=Adaptability%20is%20a%20requirement.,and%20experiment%20as%20things%20change

Conger, J. A., & Kanungo, R. N. (1998). *Charismatic leadership in organizations*. Thousand Oaks, CA: Sage Publications.

Cooper, C. D., Kong, D. T., & Crossley, C. D. (2018). Leader humor as an interpersonal resource: Integrating three theoretical perspectives. *Academy of Management Journal*, *61*, 769–796. http://doi.org/10.5465/amj.2014.0358

Den Hartog, D. N., House, R. J., Hanges, P. J., Ruiz-Quintanilla, S. A., & Dorfman, P. W. (1999). Culture specific and cross-culturally generalizable implicit leadership theories: Are attributes of charismatic/transformational leadership universally endorsed? *The Leadership Quarterly*, *10*(2), 219–256.

DeRue, D.S., Nahrgang, J.D. Wellman, N., Humphrey, S.E. (2011). Trait and behavioral theories of leadership: An integration and meta-analytic test of their relative validity. *Personnel Psychology*, 64, 7–52.

Detert, J. R. (2022). What courageous leaders do differently. *Harvard Business Review*. Retrieved January 7, 2022, from https://hbr.org/2022/01/what-courageous-leaders-do-differently

Dubrin, A. J. (2023). *Leadership: Research findings, practice, and skills* (10th ed.). Boston, MA: Cengage.

Fiske, D. W. (1949). Consistency of the factorial structures of personality ratings from different sources. *Journal of Abnormal Social Psychology*, *44*, 329–344.

Frei, F. X., & Morris, A. (2020). Begin with trust. *Harvard Business Review*, May/June. Retrieved from https://hbr.org/2020/05/begin-with-trust

Freiberg, K., & Freiberg, J. (2018). Madiba Leadership: 5 Lessons Nelson Mandela taught the world about change. Retrieved July 19, 2018, from https://www.forbes.com/sites/kevinandjackiefreiberg/2018/07/19/madiba-leadership-5-lessons-nelson-mandela-taught-the-world-about-change/?sh=5913bc441bac

Gavin, M. (2019). Authentic leadership what it is & why it's important. *Harvard Business School Online Business Insights*. Retrieved December 10, 2019, from https://online.hbs.edu/blog/post/authentic-leadership

Goleman, D. (2000). Leadership that gets results. *Harvard Business Review, March April*, 79–90.

Grant, A. (2010). Analyzing effective leaders: Why extraverts are not always the most successful bosses. *Knowledge at Wharton*. Retrieved November 23, 2010, from https://knowledge.wharton.upenn.edu/podcast/knowledge-at-wharton-podcast/analyzing-effective-leaders-why-extraverts-are-not-always-the-most-successful-bosses/

Hogan Assessments (2023). Leadership in Africa: The past, present, and future. https://www.hoganassessments.com/blog/leadership-in-africa/#:~:text=Personality%20Characteristics%20of%20African%20Leaders&text=%E2%80%9CAfrican%20leaders%20tend%20to%20excel,emphasized%20African%20adaptability%20and%20resilience

Hülsheger, U. R., Alberts, H. J., Feinholdt, A., & Lang, J. W. (2013). Benefits of mindfulness at work: The role of mindfulness in emotion regulation, emotional exhaustion, and job satisfaction. *Journal of Applied Psychology*, *98*(2), 310–325.

Judge, T. A., Bono, J. E., Ilies, R., & Gerhardt, M. W. (2002). Personality and leadership: A qualitative and quantitative review. *Journal of Applied Psychology*, *87*, 765–780. https://doi.org/10.1037/0021-9010.87.4.765

Kirkpatrick, S. A., & Locke, E. A. (1991). Leadership: Do traits matter? *Academy of Management Executive*, *5*, 48–60.

Kong, D. T., Cooper, C. D., & Sosik, J. J. (2019). The state of research on leader humor. *Organizational Psychology Review*, *9*, 3–40. https://doi.org/10.1177/2041386619846948

Korn Ferry (2023). What's the relationship between emotional intelligence and leadership? https://www.kornferry.com/insights/featured-topics/leadership/relationship-between-emotional-intelligence-and-leadership

Lituchy, T. R., Galperin, B. L., & Punnett, B. J. (2017). *LEAD: Leadership effectiveness in Africa and the African Diaspora*. New York, NY: Palgrave McMillan.

Lowe, J. (2022). Nelson Mandela: How to be a true leader. *Forbes*. Retrieved March 22, 2022, from https://www.forbes.com/sites/forbescoachescouncil/2022/03/22/nelson-mandela-how-to-be-a-true-leader/?sh=274509737535

Mayer, J. D., Caruso, D. R., & Salovey, P. (1999). Emotional intelligence meets traditional standards for an intelligence. *Intelligence*, *27*(4), 267–298. https://doi.org/10.1016/S0160-2896(99)00016-1

Mtumane, Z., & Bobelo, N. (2008). Nelson Rholihlahla Mandela: Personality traits as depicted in selected isiXhosa poetry. *South African Journal of African Languages*, *28*(2), 115–125. https://doi.org/10.1080/02572117.2008.10587307

Muchiri, M. (2011). Leadership in context: A review and research agenda for sub-Saharan Africa. *Journal of Occupational and Organizational Psychology*, *84*(3), 440–452.

Odinaka, I. (2022). 5 Skills African employers are looking for today. Retrieved August 1, 2022, from https://www.afterschoolafrica.com/50726/5-skills-african-employers-are-looking-for-today/

Senaji, T. A., Metwally, E., Sejjaaka, S., Puplampu, B. B., Michaud, J., & Adedoyin-Rasaq, H. (2014). LEAD - Leadership effectiveness, motivation, and culture in Africa: Lessons from Egypt, Ghana, Kenya, Nigeria, and Uganda. *Canadian Journal of Administrative Sciences*, *31*, 228–244.

Seibert, S. E., Kraimer, M. L., & Crant, J. M. (2001). What do proactive people do? A longitudinal model linking proactive personality and career success. *Personnel Psychology*, *54*, 845–874. https://doi.org/10.1111/j.1744-6570.2001.tb00234.x

Wanasika, I., Howell, J.P. Litrell, R., & Dorfman, P. (2011). Managerial leadership and culture in Sub-Saharan Africa. *Journal of World Business*, *46*, 234–241.

Zaccaro, S., Green, J. P., Dubrow, S., & Koize, M. (2018). Leader individual differences, situational parameters, and leadership outcomes: A comprehensive review and integration. *Leadership Quarterly*, *29*, 2–43.

3 Leadership behaviours and styles

Chapter summary

This chapter identifies the key leadership dimensions of initiating structure and consideration. It also discusses relationship-related behaviours and task-related characteristics of effective leaders. The chapter then provides an overview of several leadership styles. Finally, the chapter concludes by discussing how to select the most appropriate leadership style given the overall organisational context, expands on the theory of individualised leadership, and identifies effective leadership styles in Africa.

Learning objectives

After studying this chapter, you should be able to do the following:

- Identify the key leadership dimensions of initiating structure and consideration.
- Discuss the main relationship-related behaviours characteristic of effective leaders.
- Discuss the main task-related behaviours characteristic of effective leaders.
- Identify the main leadership styles.
- Discuss how to select the most appropriate leadership style.
- Explain how the theory of individualised leadership contributes to our understanding of leaders and followers.
- Identify effective leadership styles in Africa.

DOI: 10.4324/9781003020523-3

Mossadeck Bally is the founder of the Azalaï hotel chain in Mali, Guinea, Burkina Faso, Benin, and soon in other countries of West Africa. Azalaï is one of the rare 100% African hotel chains established on the continent. Bally began his career in the hotel industry in 1993 with the purchase of the Grand Hôtel de Bamako, which was for sale by the government of Mali, a landlocked country in West Africa. With only around ten million for the project of Bally's savings, his bank agreed to lend him one billion Communauté Financière Africaine (CFA) francs (Azalaï, 2023). He proceeded to renovate the purchased hotel to meet customer expectations. Since then, Bally has expanded his hotel chain throughout West Africa.

When Bally was asked why he proceeded with the business despite the landscape of uncertainty, Bally responded, "That's where leadership comes in ... A leader is someone who wants, who believes and who is willing to have an impact" (The Darden Report, 2020). In his vision for the new standard of hospitality, he also considered the impact on a variety of stakeholders, including the generation of young people in Africa who could potentially gain access to the career ladder. In 2015, Azalaï opened its own hospitality school to train young people for positions in the hospitality industry. In addition, Bally is part of a business leaders' organisation called the West African Business Network. The organisation created a Mali Business Angels program to provide youth with the coaching, mentoring, training, and management expertise that will help them at the start (Toulmin & Soulé, 2020). Overall, Bally summarised that his key leadership lessons were: have a vision, be resilient, be humble, be patient, and invest in people.

Our chapter identifies the key leadership dimensions of initiating structure and consideration and discusses the main task-related and relationship-related behaviours characteristic of effective leaders. Bally engaged in task-related attitudes and behaviours, such as (1) setting direction for his newly purchased hotel; (2) establishing high-performance standards to meet customer expectations; (3) participating in risk-taking; and (4) executing a plan to expand the hotel chain. Additionally, it is likely that Bally engaged in relationship-related attitudes and behaviours (e.g., aligning people and promoting principles and values) when planning to hire a generation of young people in Africa, especially since he values coaching, mentoring, training and management expertise, and one of his leadership lessons is investing in people. Finally, the chapter concludes by discussing the importance of selecting the most appropriate leadership style, explains how the theory of individualised leadership broadens our understanding of leaders and followers, and identifies effective leadership styles in Africa.

Behavioural approaches

Ohio State Studies: The role of consideration and initiating structure

Given the limitations of the trait approach, researchers began investigating key leadership behaviours. In the 1950s, studies at **Ohio State University** (known as the Ohio State Studies) became the foundation for most research on leadership behaviour, attitudes, and styles (Schriesheim & Bird, 1979). These studies identified specific dimensions of leader behaviour by narrowing down a list of 2,000 leader behaviours to 150 examples and found that two main leadership dimensions accounted for 85% of leadership behaviours: consideration and initiating structure (Hemphill & Coons, 1957).

Consideration refers to the degree to which the leader creates an environment of emotional support, warmth, friendliness, and trust. By being friendly, approachable, looking out for the welfare of the group, and doing favours for the group, the leader creates a supportive environment. Leaders who score high on the consideration dimension are friendly, trustworthy, earn respect, and have a friendly relationship with team members. Conversely, leaders who score low on the consideration dimension are often authoritarian and have impersonal relations with team members.

Initiating structure refers to organising and defining relationships in the group by participating in activities such as appointing tasks, identifying procedures to be followed, scheduling work, and clarifying expectations for group members. When leaders help group members establish realistic goals, they are engaging in initiating structure. Leaders who score high on this dimension work at establishing well-defined channels of communication and accomplishing the work required.

In general, many leaders exhibit both consideration and initiating structure behaviours. That is, these two dimensions are independent of each other. A leader can score high on both consideration and initiating structure or score low on both dimensions. Alternatively, a leader can score high on consideration and low on initiating structure or low on consideration and high on initiating structure.

University of Michigan Studies

Studies at the University of Michigan adopted a different approach by comparing the behaviour of effective and ineffective supervisors (Likert, 1979). The effectiveness of the leader was determined by the productivity of the subordinate group. Based on the findings, two dimensions of leadership behaviours were identified: employee-centred and job-centred.

Employee-centred leaders focus on the human needs of their subordinates. Employee-centred behaviours emphasise leader support and interaction facilitation. That is, employee-centred leaders not only support their subordinates but also encourage positive reactions among their followers and focus on reducing conflict. Employee-centred leadership corresponds to the dimension of consideration.

Job-centred leaders focus on activities related to scheduling, accomplishing tasks, and achieving efficiency. Job-centred behaviours focus on goal emphasis and work facilitation. Job-centred leadership corresponds to the dimension of initiating structure.

While there are similarities between the Ohio State Studies and the University of Michigan Studies in that both studies proposed dimensions, Michigan researchers viewed employee-centred leadership and job-centred leadership to be distinct styles in opposition to each other. In other words, a leader can either be identified as an employee-centred leader or a job-centred leader but not both.

Blake–Mouton Leadership Grid

Building on the Ohio State studies and University of Michigan Studies, **the Leadership Grid** integrates the employee-centred and job-centred aspects of the behavioural approach in a two-dimensional grid format. By plotting scores from leadership styles surveys, one can see where their leadership style falls on the grid (Blake & McCanse, 1991). The grid shows five main leadership styles.

The five leadership styles are as follows:

- Authority-Compliance Management: 9,1: A heavy emphasis on task and job requirements, less emphasis on the people in the company, controlling, demanding, and overpowering. This approach occurs when efficiency in operations is the main orientation.
- Country-Club Management 1,9: Low concern for company tasks and production, main concern for emotional needs of employees and interpersonal relationships, personal and social needs are met, above all, agreeable, and eager to help, and comforting. There is attention to the needs of people for satisfying relationships. This leads to a comfortable, friendly organisation atmosphere, and work tempo.
- Impoverished Management 1,1: Not concerned with either tasks or employees' needs, goes through the motions only, uninvolved, withdrawn, noncommittal, and apathetic. Exertion of minimum effort gets work done. This style is appropriate to sustain organisational membership.

- Middle of the Road Management 5,5: A compromiser, concern for task and people, finds balance between the needs of the people and emphasises work requirements, avoids conflict, moderate levels of both productions and relationships, and middle ground. Adequate organisational performance is possible through balancing the necessity to get work out with maintaining morale of people at a satisfying level.
- Team Management 9,9: Places strong emphasis on both tasks and interpersonal relationships, promotes high degree of participation and teamwork and satisfies needs of employees, stimulates participation, acts determined, gets issues out into the open, makes priorities clear, follows through, enjoys working, and open minded. Work is accomplished by committed people, and the interdependence through a common organisational goal leads to relationships of trust and respect. Refer to the MindTools website (MindTools.com) for the Leadership Grid.

(MindTools, 2024)

Overall, the literature supports that these two dimensions are the most important behaviours to leadership. In line with the Leadership Grid theory, both dimensions exist when individuals collaborate to achieve a task. In addition, leaders are able to learn new leadership behaviours with some practice. While the theory proposes that the best leaders excel in both dimensions, exceptions exist as we will see in Chapter 4 when Contingency and Situational leadership approaches are further discussed. In essence, it is crucial to assess the context in order to help better determine which style best suits the given situation.

Leadership styles

A leader's attitudes and behaviours (e.g., task vs. consideration) result in a consistent approach when dealing with group members, contributing to an understanding of our leadership style. **Leadership style** is a relatively consistent pattern of behaviour that characterises a leader. For example, Nelson Mandela, Julius Nyerere, and Ellen Johnson-Sirleaf have been described as possessing characteristics associated with charismatic leadership styles.

Moreover, it is important to note that personality traits influence which leadership style most comfortably fits the individual. For example, a leader who scores high on enthusiasm, passion, optimism, and warmth may be more inclined to display employee-centred leadership. Research suggests that (1) people who score high on honesty-humility are more likely to be ethical leaders; (2) people who score high on extraversion are more likely to be charismatic leaders; and (3) people who score high on conscientiousness are more like to be task-oriented leaders (de Vries, 2012).

We now discuss the following styles: participative leadership, autocratic leadership, servant leadership, entrepreneurial leadership, and transformational leadership.

Participative leadership

Participative leaders share decision-making with group members. The participative leadership style encompasses other styles, including shared leadership, collaborative leadership, and team leadership. Participative leadership can further be separated into the following subgroups: consultative, consensus, and democratic leadership styles.

Consultative leaders confer with other group members before making a decision, though they ultimately make the final decision. **Consensus leaders** attempt to get consensus. These leaders promote group discussion about a concern and then make the decision which is in line with the general agreement of the group. **Democratic leaders** give final authority to the group by gathering the group's opinion and then take a vote before making a decision. When employees are provided with too little direction or are being extremely macro-managed, this style refers to the laissez-faire leadership.

Table 3.1 lists the key aspects of the participative style of leadership.

Table 3.1 The participative leadership style

• Welcoming ideas from subordinates is essential as organisations become more decentralised and front-line employees have more independence.
• Key behaviours include: coaching team members, negotiating employee demands, and collaboration with group members.
• Preferable for managing competent people who want to assume responsibility, engage in decision-making, and provide feedback to upper management.

Source: Based on Collar (2013).

Autocratic leadership

Conversely, **autocratic leaders** retain most of the authority, make decisions confidently, assume that group members will conform, and are not overly concerned with the opinions of group members towards a decision. Autocratic leaders are seen as task-oriented because they place a lot of importance on finishing tasks. Table 3.2 lists the key aspects of autocratic style of leadership.

Table 3.2 The autocratic leadership style

• When a quick decision is essential, such as a crisis, authoritarian leadership may be preferable.
• Key behaviours include: telling people what to do, asserting authority, and serving as a role model to team members.
• Preferable for managing people with low self-motivation, jobs that have a high degree of complexity or technical requirements, and work environments that require following precise specifications (military, police, or fire services).

Source: Based on HRDQ (2022).

Autocratic leadership is also known as authoritarian leadership. With this approach, a supervisor has complete control over a group and the decisions made for that group—an autocratic leader rarely requires input or suggestions from their team.

Servant leadership style

More recently, the servant leadership style has gained popularity. Developed by Robert K. Greenleaf, servant leadership is a non-traditional leadership philosophy, consisting of a set of behaviours and practices that place the primary emphasis on the well-being of those being served. **Servant leaders** serve constituents by working on their behalf to help them achieve their goals, not the leader's own goals. While traditional leadership often emphasises the accumulation and exercise of power by one at the 'top of the pyramid,' servant leadership prioritises the development and optimal performance of individuals, with the servant leader sharing power (Robert K. Greenleaf Center for Servant Leadership, 2023).

There are several benefits of servant leadership which include: increased levels of trust; a positive work environment; improved collaborative efforts; and sustainable growth and success. These factors can improve organisational productivity, performance, and profits, while supporting the growth and well-being of employees (Tenney, 2023).

However, servant leadership is not without its challenges. Retraining existing leaders to embrace a servant leadership style can be demanding and time-consuming given the inherent difficulty in achieving a high level of authenticity. Table 3.3 lists the key aspects of the servant leadership style.

Table 3.3 The servant leadership style

• If you have a desire to work towards the greater good or inspire your employees to make an impact, servant leadership may be preferable.
• Common characteristics of servant leadership include: appreciation, a caring attitude, humility, strong listening skills, and a high degree of trust.
• Servant leadership proves highly effective in motivating younger employees, particularly those belonging to Generation Z. This style aligns seamlessly with their core priorities: diversity and inclusion, a healthy work–life balance, and professional development. Moreover, it serves as an effective strategy for millennials, meeting their need for respect, community, and an improved work–life balance.

Source: Based on Tenney (2023).

Entrepreneurial leadership style

The entrepreneurial leadership style involves organising and motivating a group of people to achieve a common objective through innovation, risk optimisation, taking advantage of opportunities, and managing the dynamic organisational environment. **Entrepreneurial leaders** are task-oriented and charismatic individuals.

Table 3.4 provides the main points of the entrepreneurial leadership style.

Table 3.4 The entrepreneurial leadership style

• When the context is dynamic and rapidly changing, entrepreneurial leadership is preferable since entrepreneurial leaders look for new opportunities and ways to innovate as individuals and as part of a team.
• Key characteristics include: innovative and sense of envisioning; achievement-driven engaging in brainstorming, mind mapping, and idea generation; action-oriented using their gut, intuition, and instinct; authentic, committed, and passionate; collaborative; possessing a growth mindset; determined; and optimistic.
• Preferable for managing people who are flexible, teams that are comfortable with uncertainty; and job contexts that are dynamic and rapidly changing.

Source: Indeed (2023).

Transformational leadership style

A transformational leadership style is characterised by the ability to bring about significant change in both the followers and the organisation (Daft, 2023). This style differs from a transactional leadership style which focuses on a transaction or exchange process between leaders and followers. **Transformational leaders** bring about positive and major changes in organisations. A transformational leadership style inspires employees to strive beyond required expectations to work towards a shared vision, whereas transactional leadership focuses more on extrinsic motivation for the performance of specific job tasks and is a transaction or exchange process between leaders and followers. **Transactional leaders** recognise followers' needs and desires and then classify how those needs and desires will be satisfied in the exchange for meeting specified objectives.

Transformational leaders work with their employees to implement effective change and depend on skills such as communication, charisma, adaptability, and empathetic support. Table 3.5 lists the key aspects of the transformational leadership style.

Up to now, we have been discussing key leadership behaviours and styles of effective leaders. These traditional trait and behaviour theories assume that leaders adopt a general leadership style that is used with all group members. Individualised leadership, a more recent approach to leadership behaviour research, examines the specific relationship between a leader and each individual follower (Yammarino & Dansereau, 2002). Next, the theory of individualised leadership is discussed.

Table 3.5 The transformational leadership style

- When organisations do not seem to have collective enthusiasm for a product or employees are not sure whether they want to commit into a vision, organisations will benefit most from a transformational leader.
- Key behaviours include: individualised consideration, inspirational motivation, idealised influence, and intellectual stimulation.
- Preferable for managing people who strive to go beyond required expectations to work towards a shared vision, employees who are effectively able to communicate their concerns and needs in order to receive adequate support from the leader, and employees who are open at taking risks and providing their input and ideas.

Source: Based on Dvir, Eden, Avolio and Shamir (2002); Daft (2023); Barling, Weber & Kelloway (1996); Wang & Howell (2010); Lin, Scott & Matta (2019).

Individualised leadership

Based on the perspective that a leader develops unique relationships with each subordinate or group member, **individualised leadership** posits that leader–group member relationships will determine how the leader behaves towards the member and how the member responds to the leader. Consequently, leadership can be viewed as a series of dyads or series of two-person interactions. The dyadic view examines the concept of exchange, what each party gives to and receives from the other (Dansereau, 1995).

Specifically, the leader–member exchange model, developed by George Graen and associates, explains why one sub-group can be a part of a cohesive team but another group is excluded (Graen & Cashman, 1975). **The leader–member exchange (LMX) model** proposes that leaders develop unique working relationships with group members. On the one hand, the in-group is given additional rewards, responsibility, and trust in exchange for their loyalty and performance and becomes part of a smoothly functioning team. On the other hand, the out-group employees are treated according to a more formal understanding of leader–group relations. As a result, the out-group members are less likely to experience good teamwork.

Strengths and limitations of the behavioural approach

The behavioural theory has many advantages, largely based on the view that leaders can learn and decide what actions they want to implement to become the kind of leader they want to be. Unlike the trait-based perspective, the behavioural approach is broader and allows leaders to be flexible and adapt based on their circumstances. More specifically, the strengths of the behavioural approach are as follows. First, the behavioural approach provides a broad perspective of leadership research to include behaviours of leaders and what they do in various situations. Second, the approach has been substantiated and validated by research by providing a range of behaviours related to the leadership process. Third, the approach provides the basis of identifying the key leadership styles, which are grounded in two types of behaviours (task and relationship). During the leadership process, the leader displays both behaviours during the leadership process. Balancing these two behaviours is the foundation to understanding leadership. Finally, the behavioural approach highlights the complexities of leadership and stresses the importance that the leader understands himself/herself and how others view the leader. The behavioural approach also has weaknesses. First, this approach does not focus on the relationship between a leader's behaviour and performance outcomes. Second, there is no proven successful behaviour identified with the behavioural approach. Finally, the approach suggests that the most effective leadership style is high task and high relationship. However, there is only limited support for this assumption, since this view does not take into account other situations that may need different leadership combinations (Northouse, 2016).

Leadership behaviours and styles in Africa

Overall, the behavioural approaches, including the Ohio State Studies, University of Michigan Studies, and Blake–Mouton Leadership Grid, were developed in the West. Similarly, much of the research on leadership styles has been conducted in the West. As noted in Chapter 1, one stream of research on leadership in Africa has examined the transferability of Western theories to the African context. Based on the employee-centred leader and job-centred leadership behavioural dimensions, Oni's (2017) qualitative study examined the applicability of the task-oriented and/or relationship-oriented leadership styles to Nigeria. The research explored which styles were used most often by Nigerian organisational leaders. The results show that while people advocate a fair combination of the two (based on the situation), respondents noted that most Nigerians actually use the task-oriented approach because of prevailing Nigerian work culture. Similarly, Folarin (2021) argues that democratic or participative leadership styles are preferred among Sub-Saharan African employees, citing their associated benefits, including improved performance.

A number of studies have also examined transformational and transactional leadership styles in Africa. Walumba, Orwa and Wang's (2005) cross-cultural study found a positive relationship between transformational leadership and two outcomes (organisational commitment and job satisfaction) in both cultures. Shokane, Stanz, and Slabbert (2004) found that leaders displayed a combination of transactional and transformational leadership in South African organisations, with a shift towards transformational leadership practices. However, Shahin and Wright (2004) found significant differences between the factor structure of transformational leadership reported in the USA and Egypt. These findings suggest that notions of transformational leadership do not easily translate to the African context. The authors suggest that the differences in the factor structure may be related to the construct of *asabiya* or group feeling seen in Egyptian culture (Sidani, 2008). Even though *asabiya* was discussed in earlier writings almost 800 years ago, the importance of the construct can be seen in leadership in North Africa today among Bedouins.

The LMX model can also apply to the African context. While African countries are largely collectivist, there are many different tribes or ethnic groups, which very often conflict with each other. The internal dynamics of how tribes function (with respect to loyalty, identification, reciprocity, and devotion) and strong non-contractual norms (Ouchi, 1980) could influence LMX relations in African organisations.

Research has also examined servant leadership in Africa. Hale and Fields (2007) examined the applicability of the servant leadership framework in Ghana and the USA. Their findings suggest that Ghanaians experience servant leadership behaviours significantly less than North Americans. Compared to North Americans, vision had a significantly stronger relationship with leader effectiveness for Ghanaians; however, a similar relationship was found between service, humility, and leader effectiveness for both samples. Brubaker (2013) explored the relationship between servant leadership, the African concept of *Ubuntu*, and perceived leader effectiveness in Rwanda and found that servant and *Ubuntu*-related leadership were related to greater leader effectiveness. In addition, servant leadership and *Ubuntu* were not significantly different in the strength of their relationships with leader effectiveness. Finally, there is mixed evidence for the discriminant validity of *Ubuntu*-related leadership as a construct distinct from servant leadership. We will now expand on *Ubuntu* as a leadership style.

Ubuntu-related leadership

Unlike the other leadership styles discussed in this chapter, the *Ubuntu*-related leadership style is a culturally oriented indigenised model of leadership. In indigenised models of leadership, the concept of Afro-centricity promotes a moral and spiritual transformation in African culture to reintroduce principles of communalism, participation, and connectedness to African people, thereby producing a uniquely African leadership style (Murithi, 2008).

An ***Ubuntu-related leadership style*** is characterised by leaders who demonstrate *Ubuntu* principles and empower others to act and nurture their growth and creativity, through mentoring and building relationships. Similar to transformational leadership and servant leadership, an *Ubuntu*-related leadership style is a value-based leadership, since these leadership behaviours are all primarily driven by ethical values (Poovan, Du Toit and Engelbrecht, 2006). Value-based leaders have the ability to create a value-based culture within the team (Nzimakwe, 2014).

According to Poovan et al. (2006), leaders should develop a value-based style of leading which incorporates the social values of *Ubuntu*. That is, an *Ubuntu*-related leadership style should be based on Afro-centric leadership constructs, founded on an inclusive *Ubuntu* based value system, which would include the collectivist notion of the interdependence of people in the workplace. ***Ubuntu*-related leaders** focus on teamwork, creative cooperation, open communication, attention to relationships, and reciprocal moral obligations. This approach also requires empathy between leaders and followers. In addition, leaders encourage team members or followers to sacrifice their personal gain or goals for those of the group as a whole (Botha & Claassens, 2010).

Paternalistic leadership style

While much of the focus on indigenised models of leadership have focused on *Ubuntu*, there has been less attention on paternalism, which is a big part of what might be viewed as African leadership. Less interest has been placed on paternalistic leadership despite its prevalence in the majority of the world (Jackson, 2016). **Paternalistic leadership** is defined as "a style that combines strong discipline and authority with fatherly benevolence" (Farh & Cheng, 2000: 91). Authoritarianism refers to leader behaviours that assert authority and control, whereas benevolence refers to an individualised concern for subordinates' personal well-being. Paternalistic leadership is still predominant and effective in many other countries, such as in the Middle East, Pacific Asia, and Latin America (Farh, Cheng, Chou, & Chu, 2006; Martinez, 2003; Pellegrini & Scandura, 2008; Uhl-Bien, Tierney, Graen, & Wakabayashi, 1990). However, it has increasingly been perceived negatively in Western management literature, which is reflected in descriptions of paternalism such as a benevolent dictatorship (Northouse, 2016).

Overall, paternalism is conducive to societal cultures where mutual obligations are a feature of what Hofstede (1980) and others have referred to as collectivism (Jackson, 2016). In individualistic cultures, where a clear distinction is made between authoritarian and democratic forms of management (e.g., authoritarian, consultative, participative leadership styles), paternalistic management "does not fit neatly into one of these slots, and if it does, fits into the authoritarian one" (Jackson, 2016; 4). Nevertheless, Aycan (2006) distinguishes authoritarianism from paternalism. Authoritarian relationships are based on control and exploitation where subordinates show conformity simply to avoid punishment. In a paternalistic relationship, the figure of authority, such as the boss, may be involved in the lives of subordinates as would be expected in a collectivist society. For instance, it would not be surprising if a boss in Kenya provides an advance on an employee's paycheck to cover upcoming medical treatment for the subordinate's child. Mazrui (1970) further proposes that patriarchal leadership can be profoundly African when it is intertwined with African reverence for age and elderly wisdom (Mazrui, 1970). The results of the LEAD project emphasise the significance of tradition, denoting it as a crucial and culturally specific component of leadership in Africa (Michaud et al., 2020). Findings from the GLOBE project further supports this perspective, which found that organisation and leadership in the sub-Saharan region of Africa was characterised as being "heavily patriarchal and patrimonial with little role for women in tribal governance. Leadership positions were based on ascribed status and respect was given to individuals who were male and/ or advanced in age" (Wanasika, Howell, Littrell, & Dorfman, 2011: 239).

Other studies have also found the importance of gender and age in leadership in Africa. A study examining the moderation effect of organisational commitment dimensions on leadership styles and effectiveness among Nigerian employees revealed that gender was the sole demographic variable with a significant impact between predictor and criterion variables. This implies the importance of being male, particularly the eldest child, in leadership roles on the African continent (Fadare, 2018).

Conclusion

Overall, when examining the leadership behaviours and styles in Africa, the findings suggest that while Western behaviours and styles (e.g., task-oriented and relationship dimensions; transactional, transformational, and servant leadership styles) have been found to be exhibited by leaders on the African continent, there is still an impact of culture seen in Western constructs of leadership such as the different factor structures in transformational leadership and/or mixed evidence regarding the discriminant validity with more indigenous African constructs. In addition, it is important for leaders in Africa to recognise and value the Afrocentric leadership constructs, such as *Ubuntu*-related and paternalistic leadership styles, more culturally oriented and indigenised models of leadership.

Discussion questions

- Provide an example of both a relationship-related behaviour and task-related behaviour shown by your supervisor. Which type of behaviour did you prefer? Why?
- Based on the Blake–Mouton Leadership Grid, which style is the most common leadership style in Africa? In your country? In your opinion, which is the preferred leadership style on the continent? In your country?
- In your opinion, what are the similarities and differences between servant leadership and *Ubuntu*-related leadership?
- How important is the entrepreneurial leadership style to African development in the next five to seven years?

Exercise 1: What is your leadership style?

This Leadership Style Questionnaire helps you better understand your preferred leadership style (authoritarian, democratic, and laissez faire). Indicate your strength of agreement with each of the following statements: (1) strongly agree (SA); (2) disagree (D); (3) neutral (N); (4) agree (A); and strongly agree (SA). By comparing your scores, you will be able to determine which leadership styles are most or least dominant.

Table 3.6 What is your leadership style?

		SD	*D*	*N*	*A*	*SA*
1	Members need to be supervised closely or they are not likely to do their work.	1	2	3	4	5
2	It is fair to say that most members in the general population are lazy.	1	2	3	4	5
3	In complex situations, leaders should let members work out problems on their own.	1	2	3	4	5
4	Members want to be a part of the decision-making process.	1	2	3	4	5
5	Providing guidance without pressure is the key to being a good leader.	1	2	3	4	5
6	As a rule, members must be given rewards or punishments in order to motivate them to achieve organisational objectives.	1	2	3	4	5
7	Leadership requires staying out of the way of members as they do their work.	1	2	3	4	5
8	Most members want frequent and supportive communication with their leaders.	1	2	3	4	5
9	As a rule, leaders should allow members to appraise their own work.	1	2	3	4	5
10	Most members feel insecure about their work and need direction.	1	2	3	4	5
11	Leaders need to help members accept responsibility for completing their work.	1	2	3	4	5
12	Leaders should give members complete freedom to solve problems on their own.	1	2	3	4	5
13	In most situations, members prefer little input from the leader.	1	2	3	4	5
14	It is the leader's job to help members find their passion.	1	2	3	4	5
15	The leader is the main judge of the achievements of the members of the group.	1	2	3	4	5
16	Effective leaders give orders and clarify procedures.	1	2	3	4	5
17	In general, it is best to leave members alone.	1	2	3	4	5
18	People are basically competent and if given a task will do a good job.	1	2	3	4	5

Source: Based on Northouse (2016). Leadership: Concepts and practice.

Scoring and interpretation:

Find your total score for each leadership style by summing the point values for the respective questions.

Table 3.7 Scoring key and interpretation for leadership style

Items	*Total Scores*
Sum the responses for items 1, 2, 6, 10, 15, 16	Authoritarian ______ Leadership
Sum the responses for items 4, 5, 8, 11, 14, 18	Democratic ______ Leadership
Sum the responses for items 3, 7, 9, 12, 13, 17	Laissez-faire ______ Leadership

Source: Based on Northouse (2016). Leadership: Concepts and practice.

If your score is:

26–30: You are in the very high range.
21–25: You are in the high range.
16–20: You are in the moderate range.
11–15: You are in the low range.
6–10: You are in the very low range.

Exercise 2: Being an authentic leader

After taking the short assessment above and reviewing the different types of leadership styles, which style feels most authentic to you? Ask yourself the following questions to better understand which leadership style best aligns with your values:

- Do I value goals or relationships more?
- Do I prefer structure or freedom and flexibility?
- Would I rather make a decision on my own or collectively?
- Do I focus on short- or long-term goals?
- Does motivation come from empowerment or direction?
- What are the characteristics of a healthy team dynamic?
- How important is it to you to act and nurture team members' growth and creativity through mentoring and building relationships?
- Should bosses be involved in the lives of subordinates?
- What role does reverence for age and elderly wisdom have in leadership in organisations?

There is no right or wrong answer to these reflection questions. Often individuals find their preferred leadership style by trial and error and experimentation. In addition, it is also beneficial to seek advice from a leadership mentor or trusted friends. Most importantly, be authentic and select the leadership style that feels natural to you and aligns with your strengths (Schooley, 2023).

References

Aycan, Z. (2006). Paternalism: towards conceptual refinement and operationalization. In K. S. Yang, K. K. Hwang, & U. Kim (Eds.), *Scientific advances in indigenous psychologies: Empirical, philosophical and cultural contributions* (pp. 445–466). Cambridge, England: Cambridge University Press.

Azalaï, B. (2023). Malian businessman Mossadeck Bally. Retrieved from https://www.azalai.com/en/blog/blog-post-4#:~:text=Mossadeck%20Bally%20is%20the%20founder,chains%20established%20on%20the%20continent.

Barling, J., Weber, T., & Kelloway, E. K. (1996). Effects of transformational leadership training on attitudinal and financial outcomes: A field experiment. *Journal of Applied Psychology, 81*(6), 827–832. https://doi.org/10.1037/0021-9010.81.6.827

Blake, R., & McCanse, A. (1991). *Leadership dilemmas-grid solutions*. Houston, TX: Gulf Publishing Company.

Botha, S., & Claassens, M. (2010). Leadership competencies: The contribution of the bachelor in management and leadership (BML) to the development of leaders at First National Bank, South Africa. *International Business & Economics Research Journal*, *9*(10), 77–87.

Brubaker, T. A. (2013). Servant leadership, Ubuntu, and leader effectiveness in Rwanda. *Emerging Leadership Journeys*, *6*, 114–147. https://www.regent.edu/acad/global/publications/elj/vol6iss1/elj-vol6iss1.pdf#page=105

Collar, M. (2013). Try leading collectively: Command and control leadership gives way to a more democratic style. *HR Magazine*, January, 63.

Daft, R. L. (2023). *The leadership experience*. Boston, MA: Cengage.

Dansereau, F. (1995). A dyadic approach to leadership: Creating and nurturing this approach under fire. *Leadership Quarterly*, *6*, 479–490.

de Vries, R. E. (2012). Personality predictors of leadership styles and the self–other agreement problem, *The Leadership Quarterly*, *23*, 809–821. https://doi.org/10.1016/j.leaqua.2012.03.002

Dvir, T., Eden, D., Avolio, B. J., & Shamir, B. (2002). Impact of transformational leadership on follower development and performance: A field experiment. *Academy of Management Journal*, *45*(4), 735–744. https://doi.org/10.2307/3069307

Fadare, S. (2018). Leadership styles and effectiveness among Sub-Saharan African employees. *The Journal of Values-Based Leadership*, *11*, 1–30. Retrieved from https://scholar.valpo.edu/cgi/viewcontent.cgi?article=1219&context=jvbl

Farh, J. L., & Cheng, B. S. (2000). A cultural analysis of paternalistic leadership in Chinese organizations. In J. T. Li, A. S. Tsui, & E. Weldon (Eds.), *Management and organizations in the Chinese context* (pp. 84–127). London, England: Macmillan.

Farh, J. L., Cheng, B. S., Chou, L. F., & Chu, X.P. (2006). Authority and benevolence: Employees' responses to paternalistic leadership in China. In A. S. Tsui, Y. Bian, & L. Cheng (Eds.), *China's domestic private firms: Multidisciplinary perspectives on management and performance* (pp. 230–260). New York, NY: Sharpe.

Folarin, K. D. (2021). Leadership styles, organizational performance and effectiveness among Sub-Saharan African employees. *International Journal of Scientific Engineering and Applied Science*, 7, 356–367. Retrievedfromhttps://ijseas.com/volume7/v7i6/IJSEAS202106128.pdf

Graen, G., & Cashman, J. E. (1975). A role-making model of leadership in formal organizations: A developmental approach. In J. C. Hunt & L. L. Larson (Eds.), *Leadership frontiers* (pp. 143–165). Kent, OH: Kent State University Press.

Hale, J. R., & Fields, D. L. (2007). Exploring servant leadership across cultures: A study of followers in Ghana and the USA. *Leadership*, 3(4), 397–417. https://doi.org/10.1177/1742715007082964

Hemphill, J. K., & Coons, A. E. (1957). Development of the leader behaviour description questionnaire, in R. M. Stodgill & Coons (Eds.). *Leader behaviour: Its description and measurement, bureau of business research*. Columbus, OH: Ohio State University.

Hofstede, G. (1980). *Cultures consequences*. Thousand Oaks, CA: Sage.

HRDQ (2022). *Autocratic leadership style: Pros & cons in the workplace*. Retrieved September 22, 2022, from https://hrdqstore.com/blogs/hrdq-blog/autocratic-leadership-style-pros-cons-in-the-workplace

Indeed (2023). 13 entrepreneurial leadership characteristics to develop. Retrieved February 3, 2023, from https://www.indeed.com/career-advice/career-development/entrepreneurial-leadership

Jackson, T. (2016). Paternalistic leadership: The missing link in cross-cultural leadership studies? *International Journal of Cross Cultural Management*, *16*(1) 3–7. https://journals.sagepub.com/doi/pdf/10.1177/1470595816637701

Likert, R. (1979). From production- and employee-centeredness to systems 1–4. *Journal of Management*, *5*(2), 147–156. https://doi.org/10.1177/014920637900500205

Lin, S. H., Scott, B. A., & Matta, F. K. (2019). The dark side of transformational leader behaviors for leaders themselves: A conservation of resources perspective. *Academy of Management Journal*, *62*(5), 1556–1582.

Martinez, P. G. (2003). Paternalism as a positive form of leader-subordinate exchange: Evidence from Mexico. *Journal of Iberoamerican Academy of Management*, 1, 227–242.

Mazrui, A. A. (1970). Leadership in Africa: Obote of Uganda. *International Journal*, *25*(3), 538–564. https://doi.org/10.1177/002070207002500306

Michaud, J., Lvina, E., Galperin, B. L., Lituchy, T. R., Punnett, B. J., Taleb, A., ... Alleyne, A. (2020). Development and validation of the Leadership Effectiveness in Africa and the Diaspora (LEAD) scale. *International Journal of Cross Cultural Management*, *20*(3), 361–384. https://doi.org/10.1177/1470595820973438

MindTools (2024). The Blakc Mouton Grid. Leading people and producing results. *MindTools*. https://www.mindtools.com/ai9k5cb/the-blake-mouton-grid

Murithi, T. (2008). African indigenous and endogenous approaches to peace and conflict resolution. In D. J. Francis (Eds.), *Peace and conflict in Africa* (pp. 288). Zed Books Ltd.

Nzimakwe, T. I. (2014). Practising Ubuntu and leadership for good governance. The South African and continental dialogue. *African Journal of Public Affairs*, 7, 30–41. https://repository.up.ac.za/bitstream/handle/2263/58143/Nzimakwe_Practising_2014.pdf?sequence=1#:~:text=Leaders%20with%20Ubuntu%20recognize%20their,their%20success%20is%20everyone's%20success

Northouse, P. G. (2016). *Leadership: Theory and practice* (7th ed.). Thousand Oaks, CA: Sage Publications.

Oni, T. (2017). Task-oriented versus relationship-oriented leadership styles: Perceptions of the Nigerian work environment. *International Journal of Economics, Commerce and Management*, *V*, 414–435. http://ijecm.co.uk/wp-content/uploads/2017/11/51124.pdf

Ouchi, G. W. (1980). Markets, bureaucracies, and clans. *Administrative Science Quarterly*, *25*(1), 129–141.

Pellegrini, E. K., & Scandura, T. A. (2008). Paternalistic leadership: A review and agenda for future research. *Journal of Management*, *34*(3), 566–593.

Poovan, N., Du Toit, M. K., & Engelbrecht, A. S. (2006). The effect of the social values of Ubuntu on team effectiveness. *South African Journal of Business Management*, *37*(3), 17–27.

Robert K. Greenleaf Center for Servant Leadership (2023). What is servant leadership? https://www.greenleaf.org/what-is-servant-leadership/

Schooley, S. (2023). What kind of leader are you? 9 leadership types and their strengths. *Business News Daily*. Retrieved February 21, 2023, from https://www.businessnewsdaily.com/9789-leadership-types.html

Schriesheim, C., & Bird, B. J. (1979). Contributions of the Ohio State Studies to the field of leadership. *Journal of Management*, *5*(2), 135–145.

Shahin, A., & Wright, P. (2004). Leadership in the context of culture. An Egyptian perspective. *Leadership and Organization Development Journal*, *25*(9), 499–511.

Shokane, M. S., Stanz, K. J., & Slabbert, J. A. (2004). Description of leadership in South Africa: Organisational context perspective. *South African Journal of Human Resource Management*, 2(3), 1–6.

Sidani, Y. (2008). Ibn Khaldun of North Africa: An AD 1377 theory of leadership. *Journal of Management History*, *14*(1), 73–86.

Tenney, M. (2023). The benefits of servant leadership. *Business Leadership Today*. Retrieved from https://www.businessleadershiptoday.com/what-are-the-benefits-of-servant-leadership/#:~:text=The%20benefits%20of%20servant%20leadership%20are%20higher%20levels%20of%20trust,and%20well%2Dbeing%20of%20employees

The Darden Report (2020). African Hotel Group CEO spotlights continent's promise during Africa Business Week at UVA Darden. Retrieved February 3, 2020, from https://news.darden.virginia.edu/2020/02/03/mossadeck-bally-africa-business-week/

Toulmin, C., & Soulé, F. (2020). Mossadeck Bally, CEO Azalaï hotels group: Africa's economic recovery plans must involve the private sector as an integral part. *The Institute for New Economic Thinking*. Retrieved October 13, 2020, from https://www.ineteconomics.org/perspectives/blog/mossadeck-bally-ceo-azala%C3%AF-hotels-group-africas-economic-recovery-plans-must-involve-the-private-sector-as-an-integral-part

Uhl-Bien, M., Tierney, P., Graen, G., & Wakabayashi, M. (1990). Company paternalism and the hidden investment process: Identification of the "right type" for line managers in leading Japanese organizations. *Group and Organization Studies*, *15*, 414–430.

Walumbwa, F. O., Orwa, B., & Wang, P. (2005). Transformational leadership, organizational commitment, and job satisfaction: A comparative study of Kenyan and U.S. financial firms. *Human Resources Development Quarterly*, *16*(2), 235–256.

Wanasika, I., Howell, J. P., Littrell, R., & Dorfman, P. (2011). Managerial leadership and culture in Sub-Saharan Africa. *Journal of World Business*, *46*, 234–241.

Wang, X.-H., & Howell, J. M. (2010). Exploring the dual-level effects of transformational leadership on followers. *Journal of Applied Psychology*, *95*(6), 1134–1144. https://doi.org/10.1037/a0020754

Yammarino, F. J., & Dansereau, F. (2002). Individualized leadership. *Journal of Leadership and Organizational Studies*, *9*, 90–99.

4 The leader's role in developing teamwork and motivation

Chapter summary

This chapter examines the difference between teams and groups and describes the stages of team formation. We also examine the nature of motivation and the importance of developing team motivation. In addition, we discuss leading team processes, which include building high-performance teams and the determinants and consequences of cohesiveness. Given the changes in the nature of work, we discuss leading virtual/remote teams. Finally, we discuss the importance of teams in the African context.

Learning objectives

After studying this chapter, you should be able to do the following:

- Explain the difference between teams and groups.
- Describe the stages of team development.
- Explain the nature of motivation and team motivation.
- Outline the factors that contribute to building high-performance teams and cohesiveness.
- Explain the challenges and benefits of virtual teams and the role of the leader.
- Describe the importance of teams in the African context.

Bethlehem Tilahun Alemu is Founder and Managing Director of soleRebels, a footwear entity, which redesigns the traditional Ethiopian "selate" and "barabasso" shoes. Alemu grew up in Zenabwork, a poor village in the suburbs of Addis Ababa, Ethiopia. Alemu's business, soleRebels, is one of the most popular and fastest-growing African footwear brands in the world. SoleRebels is an eco-friendly footwear (made from

DOI: 10.4324/9781003020523-4

recycled materials) that sells footwear in more than 50 countries across the world, including the USA, Canada, Japan, and Switzerland (SoleRebels, 2023a). In 2004, Alemu raised US $10,000 in capital from family and relatives. Using that initial capital, Bethlehem's business was so successful that she started another fashion business, Republic of Leather, that trades luxury leather products such as bags, belts, and other non-footwear leather accessories. When asked in an interview what was her greatest weakness as an entrepreneur, Alemu explained that she developed a good understanding of her weaknesses. She noted:

> I address those by building my team with people who have that strength I may lack. So I flip any weakness I may have and make it a strength. That is something that I had to work on—it didn't come automatically.
>
> (Probynon, 2018: para. 3)

Knowing her weaknesses enabled Alemu to achieve new levels of performance by conducting targeted hiring so she was able to fill the gaps with her team. Alemu continued:

> It empowers those who come on our team to perform because that's why we brought them. It also sets the pace for excellent teamwork, as we have a team where each member knows how to pull as needed. Weakness recognition, and a full embrace of that, is a powerful tool.
>
> (Probynon, 2018: para. 6)

Alemu's inspiring success story has been featured on Forbes, the BBC, and CNN. She was also described by Forbes as "One of The World's Most Powerful Women".

Our chapter discusses the differences between groups and teams and stages of team development. Alemu focused on building teamwork at soleRebels. That is, the group that she built relied on collaboration of each member's experience in order to achieve optimum success. Since high-performance teams and cohesiveness does not appear overnight, we discuss how leaders can build high-performance teams and team cohesiveness. We also discuss the role of motivation and team motivation. We then turn to leading virtual teams given the increasing importance of these types of teams in organisations since the COVID-19 pandemic. Finally, we describe the role of teams in the African context.

The importance of teams

There is an old African proverb from Burkina Faso that says, "If you want to go fast, go alone; if you want to go far, go together" (Tyner, 2017).

This saying highlights the importance of teamwork. When you work on your own, you do not have to wait for anyone or need anyone's approval to get things done; thus, you are able to work fast. However, if you want to make real advancements, working with others is a fundamental necessity. While teams may be essential to get work done, achieving high performance and team cohesion may be easier said than done.

While teams may not be appropriate all the time, most of the work in organisations is interdependent. That is, individuals and departments rely on other individuals and departments for information and resources to accomplish their work. When the nature of work is highly interdependent, a team is the preferable approach for attaining the level of coordination, information sharing, and exchange of needed resources to successfully complete the task. As one can imagine, groups and teams are based on collaboration, which aligns with the collectivist cultures of Africa, as seen in Chapter 1 when we discussed the cultural environment.

What is a team?

A team is a unit of two or more people who interact and coordinate their work to accomplish a shared goal or purpose. Team members are committed and hold themselves mutually accountable (Hackman, 2002). While a group of employees may work on a task that is related, the unit will not be considered a team unless the members share a common purpose that requires them to depend on each other. Teamwork denotes that people focus on combining their knowledge, skills, and efforts towards accomplishing a common goal rather than focusing on their individual needs, desires, and egos.

The four types of teams that meet the internal goals of an organisation are as follows:

- Functional teams: A functional team is composed of a supervisor and direct reports in the formal organisational chain. A **functional team**, also known as a vertical or a command team, can include three or four levels of hierarchy within a department. Often a functional team is composed of a single department in the organisation. For example, soleRebel's Help Center team assists international customers with issues related to purchases and shipping.
- Cross-department teams: A **cross-department team**, also known as a cross-functional team, consists of members from different functional departments within an organisation. Cross-department teams are often used for projects that impact several departments and therefore need several perspectives to be considered. By having cross-department teams, information is shared across functional areas, solutions are created for the departments represented, and new

policies or procedures are more easily developed. In particular, a **special-purpose team**, a type of a cross-department team, focuses on a specific purpose and disbands once the project is completed. These teams are created outside the formal organisational structure and play a special and crucial role in developing complex new products or services. For example, soleRebel may create a special-purpose team if they were interested in creating a new sustainable shoe with a different type of recycled material.

- Self-directed teams: A **self-directed team** consists of members who work with minimum supervision and rotate jobs to produce a complete product or service (Booth, 1994). Often cross-departmental teams may grow into self-directed teams. Research has shown that self-directed teams experience greater job satisfaction (van Mierlo, Rutte, Kompier, & Doorewaard, 2005).

Stages of team development

As we have seen above, team processes develop over time. Research suggests that teams develop over several stages, and team leadership requirements may vary depending on where the team is in the process (Gersick, 1988; Tuckman, 1965). The most used framework for a team's stages of development was developed in the mid-1960s by Bruce W. Tuckman. While several researchers have suggested variations to Tuckman's work, his descriptions of Forming, Storming, Norming and Performing, and Adjourning provide a useful framework for looking at your own team. By recognising how each stage works and the specific behaviours and feelings associated with each stage, leaders can better understand the team development processes. Refer to Table 4.1 for a description of the stages for team processes and feelings, behaviours, and tasks associated with each stage.

While the stages are presented as separate phases, it is important to note that the framework can be most helpful in recognising the team's behaviour patterns rather than categorising the team into a box or providing a diagnosis. Also, team processes are not always linear. Some teams may jump from the norming (Stage 3) back to storming in cases when there is a change of a member of the team (Stage 2) first rather than moving forward to performing (Stage 4). Similarly, while working in a high-performing team may be satisfying and rewarding, it's possible that changes in the organisational context may result in the team moving to an earlier stage or the team may successfully continue in the performing stage indefinitely. As teams develop over time, it is important for leaders to motivate their teams to accomplish the organisational goals. Next, we discuss how leaders motivate teams.

Table 4.1 Stages of team development

Stages	*Feelings*	*Behaviours*	*Team tasks*
Forming	• Excited to be part of the team • High/positive expectations • Anxiety about fitting in	• Lots of questions	• Create clear structure, goals, directions, and roles so that members begin to build trust • Defining the team
Storming	• Feeling of frustration or anger with progress • Concerns about goals and conflict	• Less polite • Frustration or disagreements	• Refocus on goals • Conflict management • Redefinition of goals, roles, and tasks
Norming	• Need to resolve discrepancies • Acceptance of others • Increased group cohesion	• Resolve problems • Meaningful communication • Refocus of ground rules	• Energy to the team's goals • Increase in productivity • Evaluation of team processes and productivity
Performing	• Satisfaction in the team's progress • Insights into process • Satisfaction in the team's effectiveness	• Prevention or solving problems in the team's process • Team roles more fluid • Differences appreciated	• Significant progress towards goals • Commitment to mission and competence • Progress celebrated
Adjourning	• Work is completed/ or needs to be changed • Concerns about impending dissolution • Anxiety and sadness about future • Satisfaction at the accomplishments	• Less focus on tasks and productivity may drop • Focus on the task as a response to their sadness • Task productivity may increase	• Acknowledgement of the upcoming transition • Focus on three tasks: (1) completion of deliverables and closure, (2) evaluation of the team's process, product, and "lessons learned", and (3) celebration

Source: Based on Stein (2013).

Motivation and leadership

Motivation is the energy that drives someone to engage in an action. **Motivation** refers to the forces within a person that affects the direction, intensity, and persistence of a voluntary behaviour (Latham & Pinder, 2005). That is, motivation examines the forces either internal or external to a person that arouse enthusiasm and persistence to pursue a certain course of action (Daft, 2023). Employee motivation impacts productivity, so it's important for leaders to channel their followers' motivation towards accomplishing the organisations' vision and goals.

The field of motivation provides leaders with a greater understanding on what triggers people to initiate action, what influences their choice of action, and why they persist in that action over time. Leaders can use motivation theory to help satisfy followers' needs to encourage high worker performance. For a complete discussion of motivational theories, refer to the *Essentials of Organisational Behaviour in Africa* textbook in this series (Punnett & Senaji, 2022).

In general, leaders can use rewards to motivate their followers. Rewards can be either intrinsic or extrinsic. **Intrinsic rewards** come from internal satisfaction and positive feelings a person receives while accomplishing a certain action. For example, an employee of soleRebels can be motivated by positive feelings of helping the environment by using recycled materials and creating an eco-friendly footwear. **Extrinsic rewards** come from an external source and are given by another person, usually a supervisor, such as pay increases and promotions. For example, employees at soleRebels can be motivated by its compensation and benefits, including the above-average salaries for all employees. That is, the company offers four to five times the legal minimum wage and over three times the industry average salary and provides hassle-free medical insurance that covers 100% of employee's and their family's healthcare costs (SoleRebels, 2023b).

Team motivation

Similar to employee motivation, ***team motivation*** focuses on the group of individuals and how their needs and goals are activated. The intrinsic and extrinsic motivation of the team is based on the ability of the team members to fulfil their needs and show commitment to the team. Some factors that motivate a team include task, structure, goals, and members (Hackman, 2002). In general, when the task is challenging, involving, and exciting, the team will be motivated. As discussed in Chapter 1, it is expected that team motivation will come easily due to the collectivist culture in Africa and an emphasis on communal solidarity and the importance of a group. Similarly, it is possible that the cultural dimension of paternalism and age factors may have an impact on the composition and functioning of teams in the African context. Overall, motivation is a key factor in building high-performance teams. Next, we discuss how leaders build a high-performing team and cohesiveness.

Building high-performance teams and cohesiveness

What distinguishes high-performance teams from other groups is that high-performance teams are more than a collection of people simply following orders. High-performance work teams implement strategy, meet goals, and need little management overseeing because they are empowered and responsible for their functional activity and accountable for performance. Since exceptional team performance is so highly valued, these teams do not accept sub-optimal performance. Although no team is the same, according to the Society for Human Resource Management (SHRM, 2023), high-performance teams share the following general characteristics:

- **Team purpose, goals, and roles:** High-performing teams are synergistic and work towards the achievement of a common goal or goals—both in the short term and in the long term. To succeed, members must know what to expect from each other so that they can commit to accomplishing goals. High-performing teams have a specific and clearly defined purpose and a well-defined set of goals.
- **Talent, skills, and work ethic:** High-performance teams start by recruiting and retaining their best talent. Effective teams possess the diverse set of skills, knowledge, and experiences needed to perform all the aspects of a project (Polzer, Swann Jr., & Milton, 2003). In the opening scenario, Alemu was deliberate in building her team at soleRebels with people who compensated for her weaknesses.
- **Incentive, motivation, and efficacy:** Both monetary and nonmonetary systems are needed to encourage high-performance teams. Over the long term, intrinsic motivators (e.g., personal satisfaction at work, interesting projects) provide the greatest impact on performance. A study found that high-performing teams give and receive appreciation more frequently. That is, the need for relatedness contributed to better performance at work because praise made members feel valued and appreciated, which can be more powerful than monetary incentives (Friedman, 2021).
- **Leadership:** High-performing leaders often complement high-performance work teams. The leaders encourage their team to maintain relevancy and meaningfulness of the purpose, goals, and approach; build commitment and confidence; ensure that team members develop their skills; manage relationships (external to the team)

and remove impediments that might reduce group performance; provide opportunities for others; and do the necessary work when needed.

- **Conflict and communication:** Conflict management is a key part of becoming a high-performance team. Open communication is always needed to help with motivation, maintaining interest, and collaboration. Research has shown that high-performing teams invest time bonding over non-work topics. That is, high-performing team members were 25% more likely to spend time talking about sports, books, and family and/or meeting colleagues for coffee, tea, and an alcoholic drink compared to low-performing team members (Friedman, 2021). For a complete discussion on conflict and communication, refer to the *Essentials of Organisational Behaviour in Africa* textbook in this series (Punnett & Senaji, 2022).
- **Power and empowerment:** High-performing teams are more likely to be empowered and are ready to develop new skills due to psychological safety or a team climate characterised by mutual trust and respect. When there is a high level of trust and respect for the skills and experiences of the team, the leader assumes more of a coaching role. That is, the leader provides the right level of support thereby enabling team members to be empowered and act freely, so they can use their best judgement to solve problems appropriately.
- **Norms and standards:** High-performance teams possess norms that promote team development and performance, including open lines of communication; early resolution of conflict; high levels of respect between members; a cohesive and supportive team environment; and a strong work ethic. Most importantly, high-performing teams must discuss and agree to their operating rules and standards, so all members are held accountable.

A characteristic commonly seen in high-performance teams is cohesiveness. **Team cohesiveness** is defined as the extent to which members are attracted to the team and motivated to remain in it (Shaw, 1981). Members of highly committed teams are committed to team activities, attend meetings, and are happy when the team succeeds. There are several factors that contribute to team cohesiveness: (1) team interaction: when team members have frequent contact, they are more committed to the team; (2) shared goals: when team members agree on a purpose or direction, they will be more cohesive; and (3) personal attraction to the team: when members have similar attitudes and values, they enjoy each other's company.

In cohesive teams, morale is also higher because of increased team member communication, friendly team environment, loyalty, and team member contribution in the decision-making process (Daft & Marcic, 2009). When teams are cohesive, they are more likely to be productive because members will experience decreased levels of stress, absenteeism, and turnover and increased job satisfaction (Gleeson, 2019). Research suggests that team cohesion and performance have a circular relationship (Carron, Colman, Wheeler & Stevens, 2002). In other words, higher levels of task and social cohesion contribute to better performances, but increased team performances also lead to increased feelings of task and social cohesion.

While cohesive groups offer advantages in terms of social support for group members, they also present disadvantages for the employer (MacDonald, 2023):

- **Group Norms:** Members of cohesive groups tend to follow group norms. Group norms are the explicit and implicit rules that govern the values, actions, and behaviour of group members. Some norms assist the group to function more effectively, such as exhibiting organisational citizenship behaviours and going beyond the call of duty. Other group norms can be detrimental such as group members in a cohesive group who are reluctant to put in extra effort to meet a deadline if the norm is to work at a steady pace.
- **Groupthink:** When highly cohesive groups make decisions, groupthink may occur. Groupthink occurs when group members are uncomfortable expressing dissenting opinions to avoid causing disharmony within a cohesive group. Opinions held by the majority or by key group members are regarded as unanimous, and alternative views are discouraged. Highly cohesive groups are sceptical of contradictory opinions expressed by outsiders and may even hide contradictory information. As a result, groupthink can lead to poor or irrational decisions.
- **Resistance to Change:** When groups are cohesive, members largely rely on each other and resist external ideas and input. This can lead to isolation and a feeling of superiority over others in the organisation. As a result, cohesive groups find it difficult to change their values, actions, or behaviours, particularly when the change is driven by external forces. Regardless of whether a member of the group becomes convinced of the need for change, he/she may find it difficult to make a change due to the strength of the group dynamic.

Building high-performance and cohesive teams is not an easy task. Leaders must have a good understanding of the type of team, the stage of team development, its team members, among other contextual determinants. Another factor the leader must consider is whether the team is remote.

Virtual teams and the role of the leader

Since the COVID-19 pandemic, there has been an impetus to work from home. According to the Pew Research Center (2022) in the USA, more workers say that they are working from home by choice rather than necessity. Similarly, research on work trends in South African organisations suggests that flexible ways of working have become the new normal. According to the Microsoft's Work Reworked project, approximately 88% at large enterprises in South Africa expect to adopt a more hybrid way of working permanently (Microsoft News Center, 2020). That is, employees would be required to work remotely linking with their colleagues through advanced digital technologies. A **virtual team** is composed of geographically or organisationally dispersed members who share a common purpose and are linked primarily through advanced information and telecommunication technologies. A virtual team may also sometimes be a global team (Townsend, DeMarie, & Hendrickson, 1989). A **global team** is a cross-border work team made up of members of different nationalities whose activities reach multiple countries (Govindarajan & Gupta, 2001).

There are several differences between conventional teams, virtual teams/remote, and global teams. First, conventional teams have a collated special distance; virtual/remote teams have a scattered special distance; and global teams have a widely scattered special distance. Second, conventional teams have a face-to-face distance, and both virtual and global teams have mediated communications. Finally, conventional and virtual/remote teams have members from the same culture, and global teams have members from different cultures.

It is not surprising that there has been an increase in virtual teams compared to conventional teams given the advantages of virtual teams. Some advantages of virtual teams are (1) lower costs: there is no need to pay expensive rent, companies can save on material expenses, talent pool is larger; (2) happier employees: increased flexibility can appeal to employees and no long commute times to work; (3) increased productivity: less unnecessary meetings so employees can get more work accomplished; and (4) better for the environment: eliminating the need for a daily commute can contribute to a cleaner environment (Deeb, 2020).

Despite the benefits of virtual teams, there are several disadvantages of virtual teams: (1) harder to manage: team members are not in one physical location and face to face conversation is not possible; (2) harder to team build: more challenging to build a team culture and engage in team celebrations; and (3) complicated legally: employment laws, hiring practices may differ from location to location (Deeb, 2020).

Nevertheless, leaders are able to overcome these challenges by following best practices (Tirakyan, 2021).

- **Use the right platforms to communicate**: When a team moves to virtual communication, it is important to use an appropriate platform for each kind of communication. While some issues need immediate assistance, others may require collaboration between different departments. For example, email communication is good for discussions that require the conversation to be referenced later. On the other hand, cloud-based platforms are useful when team members are working remotely and collaborating on the same documents.

- **Hold meetings only when necessary:** the virtual leader should only schedule meetings when needed and when all members are available. Since team members may be located in different time zones, it's possible that members may not be available.
- **Have realistic expectations on availability:** There may be multiple distractions that team members may be facing at home. Also, team members may have internet connectivity issues or may not have access to an internet connection all the time, which can prevent the employee from submitting work on time. This is especially true on the African continent with the high cost of data in Africa's emerging digital world and unreliable electricity (Daramola, 2020). Communicating realistic expectations from the start fosters trust and understanding in your virtual team, which can lead to a healthy workforce.
- **Be transparent with your workforce:** Leaders need to communicate effectively and be available to team members who may be struggling to meet deadlines. Also, it is important that leaders share the company goals and ensure that team members have a clear direction and align company goals with work strategies.
- **Be clear and concise in your communication:** Since there is a lack of nonverbal communication (e.g., body language) in virtual communication, it is important for the leader to engage in precise communication such as setting an agenda and managing expectations during virtual meetings.

Teams in the African context and motivating the African workforce

Teams and teamwork have played a central role in human lives starting with our ancestors coming together to search for their food, to lead their families, and to protect their community (Kozlowski & Ilgen, 2006). Teams continue to play an important role on the African continent. In a review of teams in Ethiopia, Abdulmelike (2018) examined teamwork effectiveness strategies in Ethiopian private and public organisations. In order to increase teamwork effectiveness in Ethiopia, the following strategies were suggested: (1) Teams in organisations should be directed towards common clear goals rather than personal goals. Consequently, leaders and managers in Ethiopia should influence teams in their organisations and motivate them to achieve common organisational goals.

(2) Teamwork philosophy should be discussed separately from politics, since most people perceive teamwork as a new government political tool to bring them to the political circle. Leaders in Ethiopia should emphasise on-the-job training and the research on teamwork effectiveness. (3) Effective and hard-working teams should be rewarded; free riders and social loafing should be discouraged in Ethiopia. (4) In line with the vignette on soleRebels about how Alemu built a team with complementary skills, Ethiopian leaders should use diversity as an opportunity as it brings varied skills to the team. Specifically, leaders should reduce communication barriers among diverse team members. (5) Organisations' should also inform leaders and team members about team effectiveness frameworks (Abdulmelike, 2018).

The literature has also focused on the importance of teamwork for innovation in Sub-Saharan Africa. African intellectual leaders have agreed that innovation lies at the heart of the challenges the African continent is facing. Innovation is needed to support local development and production. When developing and managing teams in Sub-Saharan Africa, leaders must understand the societal forces that impact the subunits (Seriki, 2007). In addition, leaders must understand that Africa's economic and socio-cultural environment (e.g., young workforce, gender inequality, and educational levels) may impact teams in the African context (Kuyoro, Leke, White, Woetzel, & Jayaram, 2023). Refer to Chapter 7 for a discussion on the key leadership issues, including gender inequality, impacting the future of leadership in Africa.

In particular, the literature has stressed the importance of well-managed teams in healthcare innovation management. Due to limited scientific progress and technological advancements impacted by infrastructure problems (e.g., frequent power cuts and poor access to water and electricity), among other diseases, malaria continues to be a health issue in Africa. According to Mbacham (2005), professor of public health and manager of the MIM-TDR Anti-Malaria Drug Resistance Network Africa in Cameroon, scientists need leadership and teamwork. He noted, "Until Africa's malaria researchers understand the benefits of teamwork and effective leadership, the continent will not be able to even begin to address the challenges of malaria and other devastating diseases that hinder its development" (Mbacham, 2005: para. 26).

The importance of teams has also been discussed in the hospital management literature. Due to the increased impact of disease, it is more difficult for public health care facilities to provide quality, patient-centred care to patients with complicated health needs. In their qualitative study in a tertiary hospital in South Africa, Waggie and Arends (2021) examined the barriers and facilitators of interprofessional teamwork among health professionals. Based on their research, barriers to interprofessional teamwork included increased patient turnover, lack of human resources, time, hierarchy, referral process, poor knowledge of the roles and scope of practice, harmful attitudes, communication inefficiencies, language barriers, and professional jealousy. Facilitators of interprofessional teamwork included increased human resources, communication technology, respect, and relationship building. Overall, this study concluded that interprofessional capacity building is needed for successful interprofessional teamwork at a tertiary level public hospital setting.

Research on healthcare management in Africa also highlights the importance of motivating health workers in overcoming the human resource crisis in the health sector. In their qualitative study with doctors and nurses from public, private, and non-governmental organisation (NGO) facilities in rural areas in Benin and Kenya, Mathauer and Imhoff (2006) found that many health workers were demotivated and frustrated by the lack of means and supplies, and inadequate or inappropriately applied human resources management (HRM) tools. Since some HRM tools may have adversely affected the motivation of health workers, it is essential that leaders focus on non-financial incentives such as the acknowledgement of their health workers professionalism and making sure they address professional goals (e.g., recognition and career development).

Overall, when examining employee motivation in Africa, it is especially important to examine national culture and/or regional geopolitical realities to better understand the motivational dynamics (Puplampu, 2012). In Nwoye's (2022) proposed Africentric theory of motivation, five sources of human motivation recognised within the Africentric perspective include: the need to protect against shame, the urge to overcome the limitations of one's birth or background, the need to compete favourably with one's age mates, the urge to avoid angering the ancestors, and the fear of ostracism. The theory also recognises the social nature of human motivation and the role of societal norms and values. In order to effectively lead in the African context, leaders need to understand an Africentric perspective of motivation.

Conclusion

Historically, teams have played a central role during the pre-historic time and continue to facilitate creativity, innovation, and enhanced performance in African organisations today. Given Africa's collectivist culture, which emphasises the importance of a group and communal solidarity, one would expect leaders to excel in building teams and cohesiveness in an organisational context. Nevertheless, the paternalistic leadership style (combining strong discipline and authority) in Africa may negatively impact team dynamics. Refer to Chapter 3 for more information on the paternalistic leadership style. When motivating their teams, leaders must not only provide their teams with monetary incentives but also focus on intrinsic motivators, such as personal satisfaction at work and interesting projects.

Discussion questions

- What is the difference between a group and a team?
- Based on Tuckman's stages of team development model, discuss the feelings, behaviours, and team tasks that you experienced during each stage of team development. Refer to a team at work or school.
- Based on the categorisation of teams provided, which types of teams are most common in your organisation or school? Would you suggest another type of team?
- What role can teams play in Africa's development in the 21st century?

Exercise 1: African Proverbs

African proverbs, such as the one that was shared earlier in this chapter, provide a glimpse into the rich cultural history of Africa but also offer practical advice on team building and collaboration among other areas of leadership that we have covered so far in this book. Select an African proverb from the list below and reflect on the following questions: How can you apply the quote to your daily life? What are the key leadership lessons? What skills do you need to develop to become a more effective leader? Write a 500-word essay.

Table 4.2 List of African proverbs

Topic	*African Proverb*
Teamwork	• If you want to go quickly, go alone. If you want to go far, go together. (Burkina Faso) • A single bracelet does not jingle. (Ghana) • One head does not exchange ideas. (Ghana)
Followership	• He who thinks he is leading and has no one following him is only taking a walk. (Malawian proverb)
Collective engagement	• Knowledge is like a baobab tree; no one person can embrace it with both arms. (Africa) • It takes a village to raise a child. (Nigeria)
Interconnectedness and unity	• A person is not a palm-tree that he should be self-complete [or, self-sufficient]. African proverb • Sticks in a Bundle are Unbreakable. (Kenya) • If you pick up one end of the stick you also pick up the other. (Ethiopia)

(*Continued*)

Table 4.2 (Continued)

Topic	*African Proverb*
Vision	• If you know the beginning well, the end won't trouble you. (Ghana)
Leadership and management	• One head does not go into Council. (Africa)
Ethical leadership	• When virtue founds a town, the town thrives and abides. (Ghana)
Servant leadership	• One does not regret having helped another. (Kenya)
Learning and critical thinking	• Knowledge is like a garden; if it is not cultivated, it cannot be harvested. (Africa) • He who asks is a fool for five minutes, but he who does not ask remains a fool forever. (Senegal)
Hard work and persistence	• An ant on the move does more than a dozing ox. (Ethiopia)

Source: Based on Tyner (2017), Mustapha (2023), and Dikson (2021).

References

Abdulmelike, M. A. (2018). How do teams become effective? A literature review and implication for Ethiopia. *African Journal of Business Management*, *12*, 501–508. https://doi.org/10.5897/AJBM2016.8189

Booth, P. (1994). Embracing the team concept. *Canadian Business Review*, Autumn, 10–13.

Carron, A. V., Colman, M. M., Wheeler, J., & Stevens, D. (2002). Cohesion and performance in sport: A meta-analysis. *Journal of Sport Exercise Psychology*, *24*, 168–188. https://doi.org/10.1123/jsep.24.2.168

Daft, R. (2023). *The Leadership Experience*. Boston, MA. Cengage.

Daft, R., & Marcic, D. (2009). *Understanding management* (6th ed). Mason, Ohio: South-Western Cengage Learning.

Daramola, Y. (2020). Africa goes virtual: Will it continue post-Covid-19? *EE Times Europe*. Retrieved September 19, 2020, from https://www.eetimes.eu/africa-goes-virtual-will-it-continue-post-covid-19/

Deeb, G. (2020). The pluses and minuses of virtual teams. *Forbes*. Retrieved May 4, 2020, from https://www.forbes.com/sites/georgedeeb/2020/05/04/the-pluses--minuses-of-virtual-teams/?sh=2a01c8233aba

Dikson (2021). 50 African proverbs that will get you thinking. *Matador Network*. Retrieved February 26, 2021, from https://matadornetwork.com/read/50-african-proverbs-to-get-you-thinking

Friedman, R. (2021). 5 things high-performing teams do differently. *Harvard Business Review*. Retrieved October 21, 2021, from https://hbr.org/2021/10/5-things-high-performing-teams-do-differently

Gersick, C. J. G. (1988). Time and transition in work teams: Toward a new model of group development. *Academy of Management Journal*, *31*, 9–41.

Gleeson, P. (2019). Advantages & disadvantages of group cohesiveness & productivity. *Small Business CHRON*. Retrieved March 5, 2019, from https://smallbusiness.chron.com/negative-effects-group-cohesiveness-21587.html

Govindarajan, V., & Gupta, A. K. (2001). Building an effective global business team. *MIT Sloan Management Review*, *42*, 63–71.

Hackman, J. R. (2002). *Leading teams: Setting the stage for great performances*. Boston, MA: Harvard University Press.

Kozlowski, S.W., & Ilgen, D. R. (2006). Enhancing the effectiveness of work groups and teams. *Psychological Science in the Public Interest*, *7*(3), 77–124.

Kuyoro, M., Leke, A., White, O., Woetzel, L., & Jayaram, K. (2023). Reimagining economic growth in Africa: Turning diversity into opportunity. *McKinsey Global Institute*. https://www.mckinsey.com/mgi/our-research/reimagining-economic-growth-in-africa-turning-diversity-into-opportunity

Latham, G. P., & Pinder, C. C. (2005). Work motivation theory and research at the dawn of the twenty-first century. *Annual Review of Psychology*, *56*, 485–516.

Mbacham, W. (2005). African scientists need leadership and teamwork. *Sci Dev Net*. https://www.scidev.net/sub-saharan-africa/opinions/african-scientists-need-leadership-and-teamwork-ssa/

MacDonald, L. (2023). Negative effects of group cohesiveness. *CHRON*. https://smallbusiness.chron.com/negative-effects-group-cohesiveness-21587.html

Mathauer, I., & Imhoff, I. (2006). Health worker motivation in Africa: The role of non-financial incentives and human resource management tools. *Human Resources for Health*, *4*, 24. https://human-resources-health.biomedcentral.com/articles/10.1186/1478-4491-4-24

Microsoft News Center (2020). New research reveals future work trends for South African organisations. Retrieved November 12, 2020, from https://news.microsoft.com/en-xm/2020/11/12/new-research-reveals-future-work-trends-for-south-african-organisations/

Mustapha, I. (2023). 30 African Proverbs and Sayings - Words of wisdom from Africa. *Ghana Web*. Retrieved January 2, 2023, from https://www.ghanaweb.com/vip/ibrahimmustapha/30-African-Proverbs-and-Sayings-Words-of-wisdom-from-Africa-37376

Nwoye, A. (2022). An Africentric theory of human motivation. African psychology: The emergence of a tradition; online edn, Oxford Academic. https://doi.org/10.1093/oso/9780190932497.003.0006

Pew Research Center (2022). COVID-19 pandemic continues to reshape work in America. Retrieved February 16, 2022, from https://news.microsoft.com/en-xm/2020/11/12/new-research-reveals-future-work-trends-for-south-african-organisations/

Polzer, J., Swann Jr., W., & Milton, I. (2003). The benefits of verifying diverse identities for group performance. *Research on Managing Groups and Teams*, *5*, 91–111. https://doi.org/10.1016/S1534-0856(02)05004-1

Probynon, J. (2018). The journey so far: Bethlehem Tilahun Alemu, founder, soleRebels. How we made it in Africa. https://www.howwemadeitinafrica.com/journey-far-bethlehem-tilahun-alemu-founder-solerebels/60760/

Punnett, B. J., & Senaji, T. A. (2022). *Essentials of organisational behaviour in Africa*. New York, NY: Routledge.

Puplampu, B. (2012). Employee motivation in Africa. In T. Lituchy, B. J. Punnett, & B. B. Puplampu (Eds.), *Management in Africa: Macro and micro perspectives*. New York, NY: Routledge. https://www.taylorfrancis.com/chapters/edit/10.4324/9780203111482-21/employee-motivation-africa-bill-buenar-puplampu

Shaw, M. E. (1981). *Group dynamics: The psychology of small group behavior* (2nd ed.). New York, NY: McGraw-Hill.

Seriki, H. T. (2007). *Teamwork for innovation in Sub-Saharan Africa*. Wiesbaden: Deutscher Universitätsverlag: Imprint: Deutscher Universitätsverlag.

SHRM (2023). Developing and sustaining high-performance work teams. https://www.shrm.org/resourcesandtools/tools-and-samples/toolkits/pages/developingandsustaininghigh-performanceworkteams.aspx

Stein, J. (2013). Using the stages of team development. *MIT Human Resources*. https://hr.mit.edu/learning-topics/teams/articles/stages-development

SoleRebels (2023a). Bethlehem Tilahun Alemu, soleRebels Founder. https://www.solerebels.com/pages/bethlehem-tilahun-alemu

SoleRebels (2023b). Our ethos. https://www.solerebels.com/pages/our-ethos

Tirakyan, V. (2021). Virtual leadership: 5 best practices to lead A virtual team. *Forbes*. Retrieved June 22, 2021, from https://www.forbes.com/sites/forbesbusinesscouncil/2021/06/22/virtual-leadership-5-best-practices-to-lead-a-virtual-team/?sh=75ee0c051f06

Townsend, A. M., DeMarie, S. M., & Hendrickson, A. R. (1989). Virtual teams: Technology and the workplace of the future. *Academy of Management Executive*, *12*, 17–29.

Tuckman, B. (1965). Bruce Tuckman's team development model. https://www.lfhe.ac.uk/download.../3C6230CF-61E8-4C5E-9A0C1C81DCDEDCA2

Tyner, A. (2017). Embracing diversity and inclusion: African proverbs on leadership. Retrieved November 15, 2017, from https://www.huffpost.com/entry/embracing-diversity-and-i_b_12912468

van Mierlo, H., Rutte, C. G., Kompier, M. A. J., & Doorewaard, H. A. C. M. (2005). Self-managing teamwork and psychological well-being: Review of a multilevel research domain. *Group & Organization Management*, *30*(2), 211–235. https://doi.org/10.1177/1059601103257989

Waggie, F., & Arends, N. E. (2021). Exploring interprofessional teamwork at a tertiary public hospital in South Africa. *Journal of Interprofessional Care*, *35*, 672–681. https://pubmed.ncbi.nlm.nih.gov/32838588/

5 Contingency and situational approach to leadership

Chapter summary

This chapter explores the contingency and situational approaches in leaders' influencing processes, appealing to leaders who believe that leadership should be adaptive to the situation. The question arises: "Which aspect of the situation should leaders focus on when adapting their leadership?" Various leadership theorists provide answers. While the contingency leadership scholars emphasise different situational aspects, they all advocate for aligning leadership style to the situation. This chapter discusses Fiedler's contingency theory, the situational theory, the path-goal theory, and the normative theory of leadership. It concludes by examining the strengths and limitations of the contingency approach to leadership and includes an exercise applying these theories to the African context.

Learning objectives

After studying this chapter, you should be able to do the following:

- Understand the relevance of contingency approaches to leadership.
- Differentiate between several contingency approaches to leadership.
- Describe the evolution of contingency approaches to leadership.
- Discuss the application of specific contingency approaches.
- Critically evaluate benefits and concerns related to contingency approaches of leadership.
- Generate contingencies relevant to the African context for leaders.

DOI: 10.4324/9781003020523-5

Francis Dufay became CEO of Jumia in 2022, when the co-founders Jeremy Hodara and Sacha Poignonnec stepped down. Jumia was founded in 2012 in Lagos, Nigeria, and employs 4,000 people across 11 African countries. Jumia, dubbed the "Amazon of Africa", is the largest online shopping mall in Africa, offering millions of products. Jumia is built around an e-commerce marketplace, called Jumia Logistics and JumiaPay. Dufay's leadership ability to adapt to changing circumstances is illustrated by the observations of Ahanotu (2023) about Dufay steering Jumia in a new direction, shifting away from short-term growth levers towards strategies sustainable over the long-term. According to Dufay, as cited by Ahanotu (2023):

> In the past, we allocated big numbers to promotions, customer incentives, Google, and Facebook. But that was too expensive. Now, we are focusing on long-term actions like building supply in key categories and extending to smaller cities. This takes time because it's about building logistics and educating new populations to e-commerce.

Dufay realises that it takes time to accomplish a strategic pivot and that he has to be adaptable as a leader to influence his employees and external stakeholders.

Vroom and Jago (2007: 17) note, "Virtually all definitions of leadership share the view that leadership involves the process of influence". When considering the process of influence, the question could be asked whether the effectiveness of influence is dependent on the characteristics of the leader or the situation in which the leader is conducting influence. If leadership effectiveness is dependent on the characteristics of the leader, then how does leaders' influence vary across situations? By focusing on the characteristics of the individual leader, are we perhaps missing a major portion of the phenomenon? This question has given rise to a specific school of thought within leadership studies called the contingency or situational approaches to leadership. According to these approaches, leaders can adopt behaviours that are almost in direct opposition to their natural traits when they believe that a new situation demands a different style (Daft, 2023). Leaders can therefore behave situationally, where they are able to adjust their leadership style depending on the situation they face. That is, leadership effectiveness is contingent upon (meaning it depends on) various factors, including the followers' characteristics and the organisational situation. When an organisation is embedded in the African context, it is important to take the local conditions into account that might influence leadership and followership interactions. For example, when leaders and followers are not from the same tribe, then leaders must be particularly sensitive to the tribal dynamics and realise that those conditions could influence the leader–follower interaction.

During the COVID-19 pandemic, leaders needed to communicate empathetically due to employees experiencing loss and safety concerns, compounded by fears of job loss during lockdowns. In Africa, the impact of the COVID-19 pandemic was particularly severe and several businesses struggled as a result of the lockdown as they were unable to conduct business. Figure 5.1 illustrates the element of crisis as one of the situational factors that could influence both leaders and followers. Other situational factors could include the culture in the organisation, the task structure, as well as systems and societal norms in the environment. In addition, as discussed in Chapter 3, the leader's style (e.g., participative, autocratic, servant) is an important aspect. Traits, such as the cognitive insight and emotional intelligence of the leader discussed in Chapter 2, can also influence the leader's behaviour. The position that the leader has in the organisation (e.g., being part of the executive team or in a lower supervisory level) will also influence the leader's behaviour. The leader's followers, including the degree of trust that followers have in their leader, can also influence leadership effectiveness. That is, followers have specific needs, maturity levels, different levels of training, and cohesion. These elements influence which leadership style is best suited to lead followers.

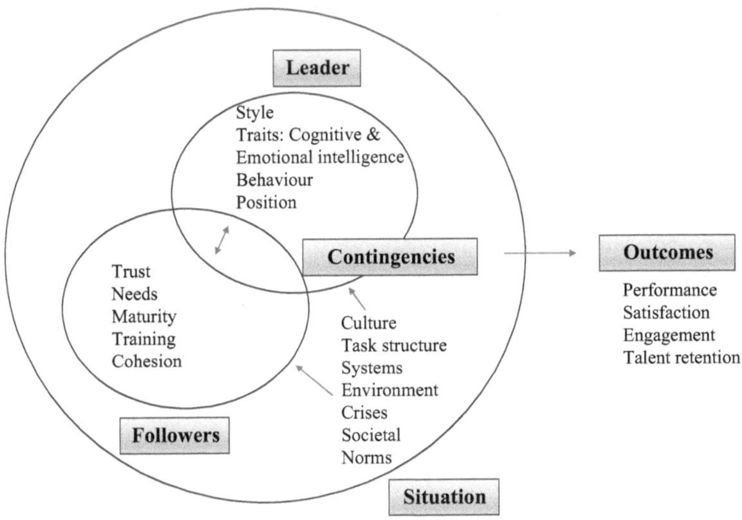

Figure 5.1 Illustration of contingencies relating to leadership.

Figure 5.1 demonstrates that several contingencies, including followers and the situations, can influence outcomes such as employee engagement, satisfaction, performance, and talent retention. Next, we'll delve into Fiedler's contingency theory of leadership.

Fiedler's contingency theory of leadership

Fiedler's contingency theory of leadership was one of the first theories to emphasise the social forces in the situation that influence leadership. In the 1960s, Fred Fiedler advised leaders to consider the degree of control the situation affords them (Fiedler, 1964). Fiedler's Contingency Model of Leadership Effectiveness proposes that a team's performance hinges on the appropriate match between a leader's style and the level of control the situation grants them.

To explain this model, it is important to consider two aspects: the leader's style and the situation.

With respect to the leader's style, we ask you to: (1) think of a co-worker that you least enjoyed working with and then (2) describe the person. Which words did you use to describe your co-worker?

According to Fiedler's initial questionnaire on leadership style, some descriptive words included: open or guarded; quarrelsome or harmonious; efficient or inefficient; gloomy or cheerful; self-assured or hesitant. Depending on how you described this person (who is your least preferred co-worker), it can be deduced whether you are a task- or relationship-orientated leader. This is an interesting feature in this model. So, if you described your co-worker using positive concepts, like cheerful, efficient, and harmonious, you are relationship-orientated. Conversely, if you described your co-worker with negative words, such as guarded and gloomy, you are task-orientated.

Fiedler assumes the leader's style to be permanent. For instance, if you describe the person in favourable terms, the **Least Preferred Coworker (LPC)** questionnaire of Fiedler would give you a high LPC score, and thus you would be relationship-orientated. Conversely, if you describe this coworker in unfavourable terms, you would get a low LPC score, and you would be perceived as a task- or productivity-orientated person. This is an important differentiator between this contingency theory and others. Since the leader's style is perceived as being permanent, the optimal match must be found between leader's task or relationship orientation and the organisational situation. Fiedler believed that this matching would ensure leadership effectiveness.

Let's pause here and ask whether you see yourself as a relationship-orientated leader or a task-orientated leader? Perhaps you do not agree with Fiedler that these are bipolar adjectives, meaning that the leader's

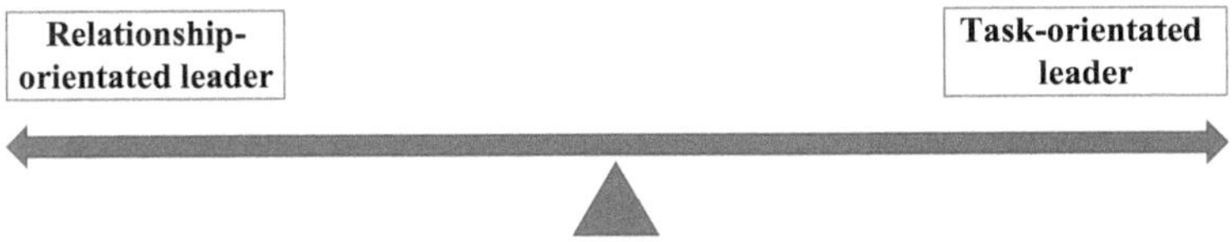

Figure 5.2 Relationship-orientated vs. task-orientated leader of Fiedler's contingency theory.

orientations are on opposite sides of a continuum? You might think you are a combination of these and that you sometimes adjust your orientation? These are important considerations that we will discuss later in the chapter when we critically evaluate benefits and concerns of the various contingency theories of leadership.

Now, let's return to the second important aspect of Fiedler's contingency theory: the situation. There are three contingencies or situational dimensions relevant in describing the situation. First is the **leader–member relations**, which describe the degree of confidence, trust, and respect that members have in their leader. Second is the **task structure**, which describes the degree to which the job assignments are proceduralised or structured. Finally, **position power** is the degree to which the leader has an influence over power variables such as selection, hiring, dismissal, disciplinary hearings, promotions, or rewards (e.g., remuneration, salary increases, or bonuses).

Putting these contingencies together, when leader–member relations are good, the task is structured, and when the leader has strong position power, the leader has greater control. According to Fiedler, a highly favourable situation is one where a leader has a high amount of control.

On the other hand, an unfavourable situation is described by low leader–member relations, low task structure, and low position power. In such situations, the leader would have limited control.

To illustrate the combination of these eight situations, Fiedler plotted the degree of favourableness and unfavourableness along a continuum.

Refer to Figure 5.3 for the situations highlighting favourable and unfavourable conditions. The figure is adapted from the original work of Fiedler (1964) and redrawn with additional explanation.

On the left side of the continuum, we see favourable conditions: good leader–member relations, high structure, and strong position power. On the far right of the continuum, we see unfavourable conditions: poor leader–member relations, low task structure, and weak position power. The task-orientated leadership style is ideal only in either favourable or unfavourable situations. In contrast, the relationship-orientated leadership style is ideal only in moderately favourable situations.

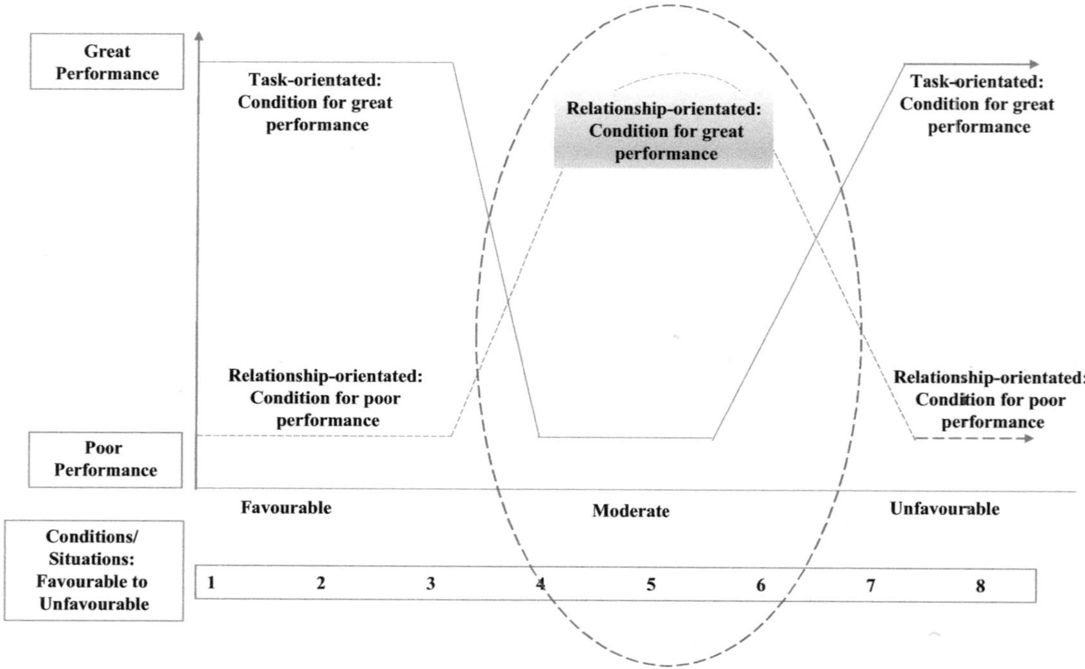

Figure 5.3 Illustration of favourable or unfavourable conditions. Adapted from Fiedler's contingency Model (1964).

The dashed-type oval circle highlights when the relationship-orientated style would be most effective for enabling great performance. For example, under the conditions of 4, 5, and 6, the dashed-type oval circle shows that the relationship-orientated style is most effective when relations are becoming poor, structure is decreasing, and the positional power varies from weak to strong and back to weak, implying that the amount of control is also varying. In contrast, the task-orientated style is most effective for creating great performance under conditions 1, 2, 3, or 7 and 8. For example, when leader–member relations are good, task structure is high, and positional power is either strong or weak, and task-orientated leadership is effective to influence high performance. When leader–member relations are poor, task structure is low, and when positional power is either strong or weak, the task-orientated leadership style is also effective for great performance.

Is Fiedler's complex theory supported by research? Initially, validity studies were supportive and sometimes partially supportive, but more recent studies are lacking. Nonetheless, Fiedler was a pioneer in taking leadership beyond the purely trait perspective and considering the orientation of an individual leader, as well as the situational variables.

The implication of Fiedler's theory is that it is better for a leader to be placed in a situation that is favourable to his or her style. An important application question here is whether you are in a situation where a relational or task orientation to leadership is best suited? According to Fiedler, it is better for you to be in a situation where your orientation is called for. The question is whether there is something in the situation that you might change to suit your orientation better? For example, could you alter one or more of the situational variables until a better fit with your leadership orientation is achieved?

Another contingency leadership theory to be discussed in the next section is the situational leadership theory.

Situational leadership

Where the previous theory of Fiedler focuses on the leader's style and the relative structure of the situation, Hersey and Blanchard's (1969) **situational leadership theory (SLT)** shifts attention to the followers. Thompson and Vecchio (2009) explain that SLT's essential principle is that employee outcomes are associated with prescribed leaders' behaviours in combination with followers' developmental levels.

That is, the readiness of followers to conduct tasks is considered to be the important contingency to consider. The appropriate leadership style is thus contingent on the degree to which the followers are willing and able to accomplish a specific task. Hersey and Blanchard (1969) described SLT as a leadership life cycle, where new employees are initially managed with more directiveness and gradually with more supportiveness as the employees gain more experience. Directiveness implies that the leader would initiate structure, and the leader would monitor results. Supportiveness, on the other hand, involves the leader displaying warmth and being considerate towards the follower.

In this regard, the followers who are unable or unwilling to do a task require a leader who gives clear direction and specific instructions to complete tasks (a telling behaviour style). However, when followers are unable but willing to complete tasks, leaders have to be highly task-orientated to compensate for the followers' lack of ability but also must display a high leadership behaviour (a selling behaviour style).

In cases where followers are actually able but they are unwilling, leaders have to adapt their styles to a high relationship orientation in motivating followers to work towards the leaders' goals and low task behaviour (a participating behaviour style).

Finally, in cases where followers are able and they are willing, the leader sometimes needs to get out of the way to allow others to take on more leadership tasks and adopt a low task and low relationship style (a delegating behaviour style).

According to this model, leaders could compensate for followers' lack of abilities and motivation. Figure 5.4 illustrates an adaptive version of the Hersey and Blanchard's (1969) SLT, where the follower readiness and matching leadership behaviours are illustrated in the same figure.

The specific leadership behaviours illustrated in Figure 5.4 are described as follows:

- **Telling leadership behaviour:** The leader gives explicit direction and closely monitors the work the follower delivers. When followers are the least mature, this leadership style with high task and low relationship orientation is most appropriate.
- **Selling leadership behaviour:** In situations requiring leaders to sell their ideas and persuade others to follow, the selling leadership behaviour of high task and high relational orientation is most appropriate. In these circumstances, followers have the ability but are unwilling to follow the directions.
- **Participating leadership behaviour:** The leader has a low task orientation and focuses more on the relational aspect of leadership, which we call participating leadership behaviour. This leadership orientation is most appropriate when followers have moderate levels of maturity and may lack the confidence to do the tasks assigned to them.
- **Delegating leadership behaviour:** In terms of Hersey and Blanchard's (1969) concept of a leadership life cycle, the final phase is where

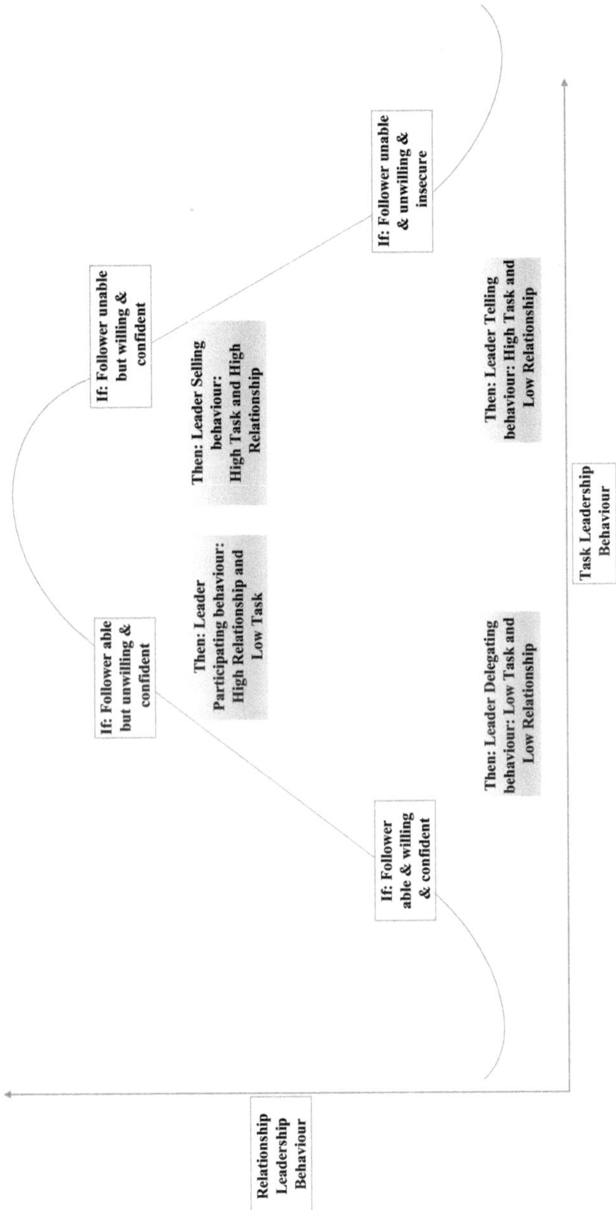

Figure 5.4 Illustration of matching of leadership behaviour with the readiness levels of followers. Adapted from Hersey and Blanchard (1969).

leaders need to exhibit delegative leadership behaviour. This style entails low-task and low-relationship leadership behaviour. The leader allows followers to take responsibility for completing tasks and making decisions. This style is best matched with followers with a high degree of maturity.

The question might be asked: When considering the level of maturity of the followers, whose criteria should be used to establish the degree of maturity? Blanchard (2010) suggested that followers' self-rating should be used in this assessment. However, what if the followers have either overestimated their competence and commitment or underestimated their self-perception of their strengths? How important would the rating of leaders be of their followers' maturity levels? Additionally, should these ratings be aligned for the SLT to be an accurate predict of the ideal leadership's behaviour, given the contingency of the followers' maturity level? Blanchard (2010) further advised that leaders and followers must partner for performance. That is, leaders should consider their followers' assessment, even if they do not need to agree. Instead, the followers' perception of the level of maturity of followers is what matters, and the leader should adapt their leadership style accordingly. Followers could benefit from gaining a more accurate perception of their development level and receiving feedback on their performance, which could come from colleagues, including their peers and their immediate manager.

To apply the learning on follower readiness, the statements below could assist in ascertaining the leaders' perception of the follower's readiness.

Consider each one of your employees and reflect on the following statements on their readiness:

Low readiness of followers is identified by the following behaviours:

- The follower does the exact work required, nothing more or less.
- The follower seems bored and uninterested in the required tasks.
- The follower takes extended breaks.

High readiness of followers is identified by the following behaviours:

- The follower is involved in extra work activities.
- The follower is recognised by colleagues as an expert.
- The follower prioritises the most important work and manages time well.

Source: These statements were adapted from the work of Daft (2023) on the situational leadership theory.

Evidence from research to support the SLT model has been lacking; however, the model has intuitive appeal. More recent studies have built on the research of Thompson and Vecchio (2009) and have taken into account the autonomy afforded by leaders and their employees' job experience in testing the SLT. For example, Thompson and Glasø (2018) empirically tested the SLT. They advised a mutual understanding between leaders and followers' maturity levels. This matching, in turn, led to better performance. These findings also support the notion that leaders should tailor their leadership style to followers' maturity levels. A higher level of agreement on the level of development or maturity of followers is conducive to an effective SLT.

So far, we described Fiedler's contingency theory and the situational leadership theory. Next, we discuss the Path-Goal Theory.

Path-goal theory of leadership

The path-goal leadership theory, developed soon after Fiedler's (1964) model, is based on the expectancy motivation theory and research on initiating structure and consideration. The **expectancy motivation theory** implies that people will be motivated when people expect the job to lead to outcomes that they perceive as valuable. According to House (1971) and Evans (1970), one component of the path-goal theory is that leaders are supposed to make rewards available to followers contingent on their accomplishment of goals. Leaders must provide followers with clarity around their paths towards their goals by offering information and supporting them in achieving these goals. The leader's function is to create and direct their followers' paths, including both individual and group goals. The leader's role is to clarify the expectations; and when rewards from the environment are lacking, leaders must supplement the environment. The types of leadership behaviours included in this path-goal theory are **directive leadership**, where a leader ensures that followers know what is expected of them by offering clear guidance, providing a schedule, and outlining standards of performance. Another type of leadership behaviour is **supportive leadership**, which includes the approachable leadership style, showing care and concern for followers and their well-being.

As a contingency theory, the path-goal theory also focuses on contingencies, that is, the "if this"... "then that" concept where the effectiveness of leadership is influenced by the situation. Specifically, Path-goal theory's contingencies dictate that the effectiveness of leadership behaviours (consideration, supportive leadership, initiating structure, or directive behaviours) depend on contingency variables, including the followers' characteristics (e.g., their abilities) and environmental factors (e.g., the task and the authority system).

When leaders' behaviours are appropriately matched to the situation, it will lead to job satisfaction among followers. Followers then accept the leader and make efforts to perform well, while also expecting to receive rewards.

When is this leadership behaviour most appropriate? In answering this question, one of the contingencies to take into account is whether tasks are ambiguous or highly structured. According to this dimension, directive leadership is more appropriate when tasks are highly stressful and ambiguous. In these situations, followers welcome directive leadership behaviour as it assists them to achieve their goals.

In other situations, when the tasks are well-structured, supportive leadership results in higher performance, since directive leadership in these situations is perceived as overly close supervision or what employees call micro-managing. In cases where employees are highly skilled and have extensive experience, directive leadership would thus be perceived as being redundant.

The path-goal theory of leadership also describes the **participative leadership** style, where the leader consults with followers, eliciting their suggestions and taking these suggestions seriously. The followers' suggestions are then taken into account when making decisions. The **achievement-orientated** style is where the leader sets challenging goals for followers and expects them to perform at their highest level. The achievement-orientated leader has high standards of excellence, focuses on continuous improvement in performance, and has a high degree of confidence that the followers will take their responsibility seriously and exert effort towards accomplishing these goals.

According to the path-goal theory, the important role of leaders is to ensure that there are personal payoffs for followers for work-goal attainment. Another role of leaders is to decrease obstacles so that the paths to travel towards goal achievement are easier and to increase the opportunities for personal satisfaction along the road to travel towards goal achievement.

The most important contribution of this theory is the leader's role of enabling goal achievement and aligning these goals with the organisation's goals. The final contingency leadership theory in this chapter is the normative leadership theory.

Normative leadership theory

The Vroom (2000) and Vroom and Jago (2007) normative leadership theory is narrower in focus than the path-goal theory and focuses on the degree to which followers participate in decision-making, which in turn influences the acceptance of the decision by followers. Leaders' behaviour must reflect the task structure (routine or the non-routine tasks and

Figure 5.5 Illustration of the continuum between decide and delegating. Based on and adapted from the Vroom and Jago's (2007) normative leadership theory.

those in between) and implies that "the way the leader makes decisions is therefore as important as what he or she decides" (Robbins & Judge, 2017: 427).

The effectiveness of the degree to which followers are participating in decision-making is dependent on situational variables. When a leader faces a problem, decisions to solve the problem might be made by the leader alone or by including a number of followers. The normative leadership theory can serve as a guide that leaders can use to assist them in deciding whether it would be best to make the decision on their own or to involve others in the decision-making. This theory helps leaders to decide on the degree of participation that is required.

In this regard, the normative or prescriptive model includes five decision processes, which fall along a continuum. The leader must choose one of the five styles, depending on the situation. Figure 5.5 shows the continuum between the leader making the decision about how to solve the problem alone (decide) and ultimately delegating the problem so that the group can take the decision (delegate).

As illustrated in Figure 5.5, the five decision processes lie on a continuum. On the one end of the continuum is the first decision process, namely **Decide**—the leader making the decision alone. The second decision process is **Consult Individually**—presenting the problem to followers individually for their suggestions and then making the decision. The third decision process is **Consult Group**—collectively gathering the followers' ideas and suggestions and then making the decision. The fourth decision process is **Facilitate**—sharing the problem with followers as a group and then playing the role of a facilitator to help the group arrive at a decision. The other end of the continuum shows the fifth decision process, namely **Delegate**—delegating the problem and allowing the group to take the decision within prescribed limits.

The situational factors, which influence the appropriate degree of decision participation, include: the required level of decision quality, the level of leader or follower expertise, and the importance of commitment to the decision (Daft, 2023).

The required degree of participative decision-making is influenced by situational variables, including the importance of the decisions to be made, the need for commitment from followers to the decision, and the likelihood of conflict. The normative leadership theory, therefore, offers a decision tree which applies rules to specific situations.

The theory also allows leaders to use their discretion, taking the timeline into account. In urgent situations, less consultation time will be available for participative decision-making. In situations where the decision-making process will offer development opportunities for followers, leaders must involve the followers in the decision-making process (Daft, 2023). Some of the decision rules include the degree to which followers have knowledge relevant to a decision. The relevant knowledge of followers would influence the degree to which these followers would be included in decision-making. Thus far, we have discussed the various contingency approaches to leadership, and the next section pays attention to the strengths and limitations of these theories.

Strengths and limitations of the contingency theories

The most important strength and learning point from the contingency theories of leadership is: "Actions must be tailored to fit the demands of each situation" (Vroom & Jago, 2007: 23). In effect, a leadership style that is appropriate for one situation might not be relevant to the next situation. The strength of the contingency theories of leadership lies in the context of the interaction between leaders and followers.

Leaders are often blamed for the lack of performance in their organisations, and the contribution of contingency theories in leadership highlights that the control of individual leaders over organisational outcomes might be overestimated. This overestimation can lead to the failure to consider the important role that the situation or context plays in leadership.

Nevertheless, a limitation of contingency theories is that specific theories only highlight particular elements of the situation, such as participation in decision-making or the characteristics of followers, and pay limited attention to other dimensions of the context surrounding the leader–follower interaction processes. In the evolution of the contingency theories, scholars have shifted their emphasis to different aspects of the context. This indicates that future studies might need to consider yet again different aspects of the context. Research on dimensions of context has mainly focused on experiments and offering respondents hypothetical scenarios to make decisions of how to deal with leadership situations. These quantitative approaches lacked the depth afforded by qualitative methods to delve deeper into aspects of the context which were not initially considered.

Drawing on the trait theories of leadership as seen in Chapter 2, the limitations of the contingency theories are centred around inadequately, considering the characteristics of the leader or the agency of the leader to influence a situation. Contingency theories intended to place the emphasis on the situation in response to the overemphasis on the individual leader's characteristics. Herein lies their limitation pointing to the need for approaching leadership from a holistic viewpoint, where both the leader and the situation within which the leader finds him/herself are considered.

An aspect of the context which has received limited attention in contingency studies is the cultural or tribal differences between leaders and followers. Next, we discuss contingencies in the African context.

Contingency theories in Africa

The typical contingencies mentioned in the leadership theories developed in the Western context may indeed need adaptation to fit the African context. While some principles may apply universally, African theorists might need to create original decision trees or guidelines tailored to unique contingencies in Africa.

One perspective is to build on existing research offering decision-making guidelines, allowing leaders in Africa to adapt their leadership styles based on their understanding of contingency theories. This approach acknowledges the universality of certain leadership principles while also recognising the need for contextual adaptation.

In Africa, the reality includes the presence of multinational companies and transnational organisations with global operations. Many of these contingency theories could remain relevant in an African context, as leadership principles are often applicable across different cultural contexts. However, there may be specific contingencies in Africa that generic theories do not fully account for.

Therefore, it's essential to consider which specific contingencies would be important in an African context considering factors such as cultural differences, socioeconomic conditions, and political landscapes. Tailoring leadership approaches to these specific contingencies can lead to more effective leadership outcomes in African settings.

In the context of Africa's rapidly growing youth population with high expectations, the Hersey and Blanchard (1982) model's emphasis on follower maturity as a situational variable may require adaptation. Intuitively, it may seem that an authoritarian style might not be suitable in situations where the followers have limited work experience. This highlights the complexity of leadership situations, where multiple dimensions need consideration. For example, factors such as the type of tasks or the severity of consequences of failure may also influence the leadership style appropriateness.

In cases where high stakes and risks are involved and wrong decisions could have significant consequences, limiting participation in decision-making to followers with knowledge and experience may be necessary. This underscores the importance of considering various aspects of the situation beyond just follower maturity when determining the most appropriate leadership style. Adapting leadership approaches to account for the unique challenges and characteristics of African contexts requires a nuanced understanding of both traditional leadership theories and the specific contextual factors at play.

The concept of follower maturity, particularly in the context of the followers' perception of their own maturity, becomes even more pertinent when considering the high power distance culture in Africa. In cultures with high power distance, followers may be less likely to perceive themselves as mature, as their cultural values emphasise deference to authority figures.

In such contexts, followers may hesitate to participate in decision-making processes, viewing themselves as lower in status compared to their leaders. This cultural dynamic adds an additional layer of complexity to the participation in decision-making contingency theory.

Examining contingencies specific to the African context allows for a more nuanced understanding of leadership dynamics and facilitates the development of tailored leadership approaches that resonate with the cultural and social realities of the region.

Conclusion

The case of Francis Dufay, the CEO of Jumia, exemplifies the principles of contingency theories of leadership. While trait theories focus on the characteristics of leaders, the contingency theories question and challenge this approach by emphasising the empirical evidence of leaders' behaviour varying across different situations. Despite possessing specific personality traits, Dufay demonstrates self-awareness and purposefully adapts his leadership style to evolving circumstances.

In conclusion, contingency and situational theories of leadership highlight the importance of contextual factors in the leader–follower dynamic. By considering situational variables, these theories provide valuable insights for both leadership studies and practical leadership applications.

Discussion questions

- Taking into account each of the contingency theories, what are the main learning points from each theory? Which situational variables are outlined by each of the contingency theories?

- Is there one situational variable that would be sufficient to consider when choosing an appropriate leadership style?
- Which contingency theories best describe your environment?
- Applying the contingency theories to the African context, what are the most important factors to consider in Africa?

Exercises

Exercise 1: Practical application of contingency theories

A well-known model in practice is the Hersey and Blanchard (1983) situational leadership model. Using Artificial Intelligence software (ChatGTP or other software), analyse the situational model. Hersey and Blanchard (1983) offered four leadership styles (ranging from telling to delegating) and suggested that leaders adapt this style to match the situation. Consider these questions: which situational variable was suggested by these scholars in this matching process? For example, when leaders must decide whether they should use a telling style or delegating style, which variable would give them an indication and which leadership style is most appropriate?

Exercise 2: Leading a team in Africa

Analyse the scenario below and then apply the different contingency theories to decide the best course of action.

You need to manage a team in Africa tasked with developing drone technology. The team consists of highly talented people, who are experts in high-end technology. The obvious approach would be to give this team a clear project with objectives and then let them decide how to organise themselves to get it done. Since the team is comprised of technical experts, they would likely prefer autonomy and one would expect that the team would prefer to be left alone to get on with the job.

Drawing on the contingency theories of leadership, what would be the best approach to lead this team? Be sure to focus on the contingency/situational factors discussed in the chapter. A discussion of this case is provided at the end of the chapter.

Exercise 3: Assessing your preferred leadership style

In terms of the contingency theories of leadership, it is important to consider which leadership style is largely required to ensure effective outcomes. The following questions were adapted from Daft (2023) and could assist leaders in identifying either a task orientation or people-oriented leadership style:

Please answer the following questions according to the Likert scale (5 = almost always; 4 = often; 3 = sometimes; 2 = seldom; 1 = almost never).

The following questions assess a task orientation leadership style.

How often do you:

		Almost never	*Seldom*	*Sometimes*	*Often*	*Almost always*
1	Hold employees personal accountable for their performance?	1	2	3	4	5
2	Assign employees to specific roles and tasks?	1	2	3	4	5
3	Check on employees to know how they are doing?	1	2	3	4	5
4	Focus more on execution than on being pleasant with employees?	1	2	3	4	5

A high score (4 or higher per question) indicates that you are mostly task orientated.

The following questions assess a people-oriented leadership style.

How often do you?

		Almost never	*Seldom*	*Sometimes*	*Often*	*Almost always*
1	Allow employees to do their work the way they think best?	1	2	3	4	5
2	Concern yourself with employees' personal feelings and welfare?	1	2	3	4	5
3	Go out of your way to be helpful to employees?	1	2	3	4	5
4	Make employees' work more pleasant?	1	2	3	4	5

A high score (4 or higher per question) indicates that you are mostly people orientated.

Given whether you are more task-orientated or more people-orientated, the contingency theories indicate that there will be ideal situations for your orientation. It is therefore important to match your style with the specific team members that you need to lead and the situation.

Exercise 4: Assessing the frequency with which you take a situational perspective on leadership

The following exercise assists in highlighting contingency. The exercise aims to establish whether you have a strong, moderate, or weak situational perspective as a leader. The following statements were adapted from recent work of DuBrin (2023). Indicate the frequency that you take a situational perspective to leadership. By using the following frequency scale (5 = almost always; 4 = often; 3 = sometimes; 2 = seldom; 1 = almost never), consider the following statements:

		Almost never	Seldom	Sometimes	Often	Almost always
1	Employees who are anxious usually need a lot of reassurance.	1	2	3	4	5
2	Employees need to be carefully trained before you can place high expectations on them.	1	2	3	4	5
3	It is best to put in much effort in supervising unenthusiastic employees.	1	2	3	4	5
4	When I notice an employee appears to be insecure and anxious, I would give them especially clear instructions and guidance.	1	2	3	4	5
5	Employees who are self-confident and intelligent require less supervision and guidance than do other employees.	1	2	3	4	5

	Almost never	Seldom	Sometimes	Often	Almost always
6 Many competent employees get to a point where they require relatively little supervision.	1	2	3	4	5
7 Whether a person is a younger or older adult often influences the best approach to leading them.	1	2	3	4	5

Scoring and interpretation: Find your total score by summing the point values for each question.

28 and above: You have a strong situational perspective as a leader.
20–28: You have a moderate situational perspective.
Below 20: You rarely take a situational perspective as a leader and might want to pay special attention to the contingency theories of leadership as described in this chapter.

Discussion of Exercise 1: Practical application of contingency theories

This scenario highlights the complexity of leadership within a team setting and underscores the relevance of contingency leadership theories in practical application. Specifically, Hersey and Blanchard's situational leadership theory (1983) suggests that leaders should adapt their leadership style based on the maturity level of their team members. In this case, where technical experts are perceived to have a high maturity level, a delegating leadership style, characterised by low task and low relationship behaviour, may be suitable.

However, it's important to note that individual differences within the team, such as varying levels of expertise and readiness, must also be considered. While the team as a whole may exhibit high maturity, individual team members may have different levels of competence and commitment. Therefore, an individualised approach to leadership, tailored to the specific needs and readiness of each team member, would be more appropriate than a one-size-fits-all approach.

Drawing from the normative leadership theory, the type of decisions and the readiness of team members to participate in decision-making should also be considered. Additionally, the path-goal leadership theory suggests that leaders should identify and align individual goals with the overall team objectives. This may involve setting personalised development plans for each team member to foster their expertise and motivation.

Overall, this case demonstrates the importance of considering various situational variables and individual differences in leadership practice, highlighting the practical relevance of contingency leadership theories.

References

Ahanotu, D. (2023). CEO Francis Dufay pivoting Jumia Amidst challenging macroeconomic conditions. *Seeking Alpha*. https://seekingalpha.com/article/4609208-ceo-francis-dufay-pivoting-jumia-amidst-challenging-macroeconomic-conditions

Blanchard, K. H. (2010). *Leading at a higher level. Revised and expanded edition*. Upper Saddle River, NJ: Blanchard Managing Corporation.

Daft, R. (2023). *The leadership experience*. Boston, MA. Cengage.

DuBrin, A. J. (2023). *Leadership: Research findings, practice, and skills*. Boston, MA. Cengage.

Evans, M. G. (1970). The effects of supervisory behaviour in the path-goal relationship. *Organizational Behaviour and Human Performance*, *5*, 277–298.

Fiedler, F. E. (1964). A contingency model of leadership effectiveness. *Advances in Experimental Social Psychology*, *1*, 149–190. https://www.sciencedirect.com/science/article/pii/S0065260108600519

Hersey, P., & Blanchard, K. H. (1982). *Management of organizational behavior: Utilizing human resources* (4th ed.). Englewood Cliffs, NJ: Prentice Hall.

Hersey, P., & Blanchard, K. H. (1969). Life cycle theory of leadership. *Training & Development Journal*, *23*(5), 26–34.

House, R. J. (1971). A path-goal theory of leader effectiveness. *Administrative Science Quarterly*, *16*, 321–338.

Robbins, S. P., & Judge, T. A. (2017). *Organizational behavior* (17th ed.). Pearson.

Thompson, G., & Vecchio, R. P. (2009). Situational leadership theory: A test of three versions. *The Leadership Quarterly*, *20*(5), 837–848.

Thompson, G., & Glasø, L. (2018). Situational leadership theory: A test from a leader-follower congruence approach. *Leadership & Organization Development Journal*, *39*(5), 574–591. https://doi.org/10.1108/LODJ-01-2018-0050

Vroom, V. H., & Jago, A. G. (2007). The role of the situation in leadership. *American Psychologist*, *62*(1), 17–24. https://doi.org/10.1037/0003-066X.62.1.17

Vroom, V. H. (2000). Leadership and the decision-making process. *Organizational Dynamics*, *28*(4), 82–94.

6 Organisational leadership and development

Chapter summary

In this chapter, we cover organisational leadership, focusing on business units and larger organisations. The role of formulating a vision and strategy for the organisation is discussed, and we delve into leadership development in Africa. We also focus on ethical leadership and offer exercises to practically apply organisational leadership development in the African context.

Learning objectives

After completing this chapter, you will be able to do the following:

- Define organisational leadership and strategic leadership.
- Describe how ethical leadership differs from authentic and servant leadership.
- Outline different methods of leadership development.
- Discuss organisational leadership development in the African context.

Tony Elumelu is one of Africa's leading investors and philanthropists. He is the founder and chairman of Heirs Holdings, his family-owned investment company committed to improving lives and transforming Africa. Elumelu is the chairman of pan-African financial services group, the United Bank for Africa (UBA), which operates in 20 countries in Africa. UBA has 21 million customers and is the only African bank with a commercial deposit taking presence in the USA. Elumelu is the most

DOI: 10.4324/9781003020523-6

prominent champion of entrepreneurship in Africa, according to the World Economic Forum (2023). Elumelu said:

> In my engagement with fellow private sector leaders, my message is simple: We must see ourselves as the engine of innovation, the source of investment, and the creators of jobs. This is exactly what we have achieved at The Tony Elumelu Foundation.
>
> (Twitter, @TonyElumeluFDN)

Elumelu was named Time100 Most Influential People in the World in 2020, recognised for his business leadership and economic empowerment of young Africans.

While some leaders focus on the leadership of small groups, **organisational leadership** entails the leadership of a company or its business units. Thus, organisational leadership is larger in scale and scope than team leadership. Tony Elumelu's leadership is an example of organisational leadership.

Organisational leadership could entail inspiring and influencing others whom the leader does not directly interact with. This influence happens through creating a vision for the organisation, developing a strategy, planning the execution, and implementing the strategy. Since organisational change may be required in implementing the strategy, organisational leadership regularly entails the management of change. Since dealing with strategy is an important function of organisational leadership, we discuss strategic leadership in the next section.

Elements of strategic leadership

Strategy is defined by Hough, Thompson, Stickland III, and Gamble (2008: 4) as "managerial commitment to pursue a particular set of actions in growing the business, attracting and pleasing customers, competing successfully, conducting operations, and improving the company's financial and market performance". Basically, the strategy aims to capitalise on opportunities and to mitigate risks in the environment of the company. Strategic leaders must, therefore, be intimately involved in exploring the environment and identifying the opportunities and risks which might impact the organisation.

To lead strategically, leaders' focus must be on the formulation and execution of strategy. **Strategic leadership** is about translating an organisation's vision into reality (Hooiberg & Lane, 2014). The purpose of strategic leadership is to cascade the vision throughout the organisation. Strategic leaders influence the organisation's values and culture (Carter & Greer, 2013). This implies that strategic leadership involves the formulation of the vision and strategy, as well as the implementation of this strategy. In *The Leadership Quarterly* (one of the top academic journals in the leadership domain), Boal and Hooijberg (2001) explain the evolution of the theory on strategic leadership. They perceive strategic leaders as those in top management positions at the strategic apex of the organisation. These leaders are sometimes called the **Top Management Team (TMT)** and in academic literature called the **Upper Echelon Theory of leadership.** Boal and Hooijberg (2001: 516) also emphasise that the top leadership in the organisation is the "dominant coalition", which runs the organisation, gives direction, and has a significant influence on the success of an organisation.

Hitt, Haynes, and Serpa (2010) describe the elements of strategic leadership as:

- developing and communicating a vision;
- building dynamic core competencies or those competencies which are at the centre of the organisation;
- emphasising and effectively using human capital or those capabilities in the organisation relating to the people;
- investing in the development of new technologies;
- engaging in valuable strategies or those strategies that add value to the organisation;
- building and maintaining an effective organisational culture;
- developing and implementing balanced controls, that is, measurements of both the financial outcomes and the operational inputs and human resources measurements;
- engaging in ethical practices.

An example of a leader who had a vision is Gert Schoonbee, Managing Director of T-Systems South Africa (TSSA), a South African subsidiary of T-Systems, which is part of Deutsche Telekom AG. Schoonbee developed the "net positive" vision in 2018 to explain that an organisation has to make a positive impact on its environment meaning that causing no harm to an organisation's environment is not adequate. Schoonbee advocated that strategic leaders in an organisation must ensure that the net result or ultimate impact on the organisation's environment must be positive. For example, technology sometimes replaces humans, and in a country with low employment rates, TSSA created two jobs for each one job that might be impacted by technology to ensure a "net positive" result. A case study on the vision of Schoonbee by Scheepers, Verachia, and Motsepe (2018) shares the story of how Schoonbee ensured that the whole organisation understood and bought-in to this vision. The idea of "net positive" was integrated in decisions, including the decision to invest in corporate social responsibility, a business model with the idea that a business has a responsibility to the society that exists around it

(Stobierski, 2021). Carter and Greer (2013) highlight that strategic leaders must focus on triple bottom line (profit, people, and planet) performance measures. More specifically, the people aspect of the triple bottom line includes the employees of the organisation, the customers, and communities impacted by the organisation. The planet aspect involves the impact on the environment, including the consumption and waste of electricity or water, hazardous waste generation, and greenhouse gas emissions. Organisations can no longer only focus on their financial performance; they also need to consider the social and environmental impact of their organisation.

This story of Gert Schoonbee at TSSA illustrates that strategic leadership is required on other levels in the organisation, not only at the top of the organisation. When lower levels in the organisation are able to think on strategic levels and willing to get involved in strategy, their contribution includes assisting in the formulation and support in executing strategy. The input into the strategy comes from a broader base, increasing the likelihood of accuracy in terms of positioning the organisation appropriately.

Strategic leadership involves complex thinking in decision-making

Strategic decisions on how to capitalise on opportunities to be more profitable in future, or to mitigate risks, require a level of decision-making that is complex, since there are more variables to take into account, and those variables have an influence on one another. When taking these strategic decisions, Nadkarni and Narayanan (2007) emphasise that the principles relating to our strategy have to be adequately complex to promote strategic flexibility. That is, strategies that you formulate for your business, such as how to capitalise on opportunities in the future, need to be adequately complex and take several variables into account, which could be interdependent, meaning that the different variables might influence one another.

Osborn and Marion (2009) note that leadership is embedded in context with a complex and uncertain reality, especially at the top of an organisation. Porter and McLaughlin (2006) state that leadership does not take place in a vacuum, and thus, we must contextualise leadership. In this book, we therefore explain the different types of leadership and how these types are relevant to certain contexts, such as the African continent. Organisational leadership functions on the larger scale of the organisation, and therefore, strategic thinking is relevant on this level of leadership.

In an article in *Business Horizons*, Hitt et al. (2010) discuss strategic leadership for the 21st century, noting that strategic leaders have to pay attention to the following trends in the environment of businesses, including hypercompetitive markets; competing across industry boundaries (e.g., telecommunication companies are competing with television companies or utility companies); and converging technologies (e.g., software companies tend to offer financial services and automotive manufacturers offer insurance and car financing). These trends are making the business environment more complex to manage and require leaders to be purposeful in managing these trends that might impact their businesses.

Strategic management process

Operationalising strategy is a source of competitive advantage, and therefore, strategic leadership focuses on creating and implementing strategy. Strategic implementation is a dynamic, iterative, complex process involving various activities by managers and employees who work to turn strategic plans into reality, in order to achieve strategic objectives. **Strategic implementation effectiveness** is the extent to which an organisation's implemented strategies correspond to its strategic intentions (Tawse & Tabesh, 2021). The business model, in turn, explains the rationale behind why a company's strategy will lead to the company increasing its financial position. Once a strategy had been crafted, a dynamic process is required, whereby an organisation's strategy is calibrated with its culture, leadership, and the organisation's structure and governance. This organisational alignment is an important strategic management process.

According to Kaplan and Norton (2006), strategic alignment between the corporate, business unit and support strategies is crucial to derive benefits from the strategy. Kaplan and Norton are well known for their **Balanced Scorecard (BSC)**, which is a tool to ensure a clear strategy map, and strategic objectives are aligned across the business units internal to the organisation and stakeholders external to the organisation. Kaplan and Norton (1992) originally emphasised that the balanced scorecard tracks all the important elements of a company's strategy, that is, from continuous improvement and partnerships to teamwork. The BSC measures what drives performance. For example, the main message of the BSC is that financial performance measures must be balanced with the customers' and employees' perspective and the operational internal business perspective.

In the exercise at the end of this chapter, there will be an opportunity to populate the figure by inserting the measures for each of the elements of the BSC. This practical exercise will give you an opportunity to consider how these measures apply to a specific organisation.

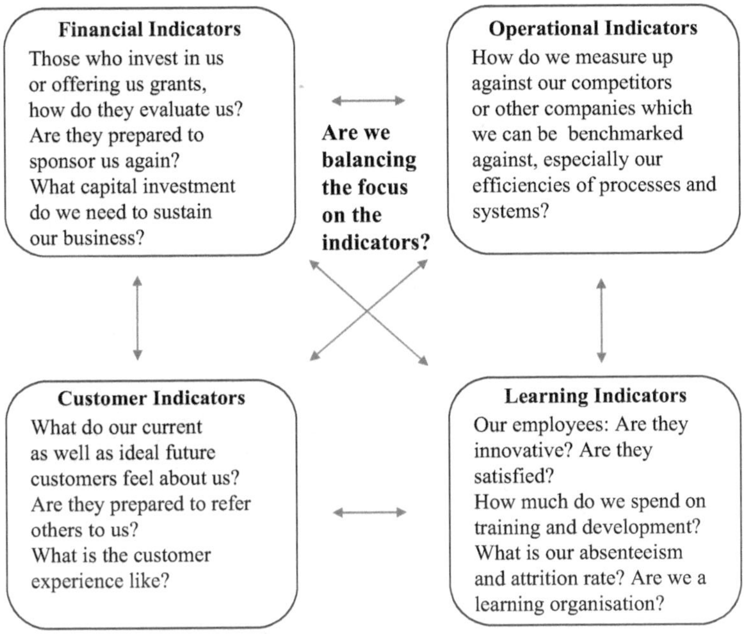

Figure 6.1 Example of Balanced Scorecard. Adapted from Kaplan and Norton (1992).

Related to the concept of alignment, Beer, Voelpel, Leibold, and Tekie's (2005) developed the term organisational fitness capability. **Organisational fitness capability** implies that the organisation is able to adapt to its environment. It requires leaders to purposefully lead a systemic organisational learning process, where the whole organisation is involved in learning. The organisational learning must, therefore, be an integrated approach that renews or rejuvenates the whole organisation. The reshaping of various elements of the organisation, such as the culture, structure, and political landscape, is required for rejuvenation.

Crafting a vision and mission statement

Boninelli (2013) offers an example of a company that is focused on systematically developing their leaders of the future. AngloGold Ashanti is a multinational gold-mining company with over 60,000 employees, with a presence in ten countries in North and South America, Australia, and in Africa, including Ghana, Tanzania, and South Africa. AngloGold Ashanti's primary listing is on the Johannesburg Stock Exchange, and their vision statement is to be "the leading mining company". Italia Boninelli (2013) shares that their company's emphasis is on people who are not only human assets, instead emphasising that "People are the Business". This aspect of leading people is intentionally ranked first among their five core strategies. It is testament to their conviction that the people working at AngloGold Ashanti are central to their success. They endeavour to achieve this vision through five core strategies, including recognising that "People are the Business" and that organisational development will be a strategic driver for the business. They want to maximise margins by managing revenues and costs. They embrace sustainability principles and focus on creating value for both business and social partners to manage risk and opportunity.

AngloGold Ashanti's mission is to create value safely and responsibly for all people. People include their employees, shareholders, business and social partners, the local communities, and societies in places where AngloGold Ashanti has a presence. This focus also draws more attention on how Anglo Gold Ashanti delivers on their vision and places importance on the outcome. Paying attention to how we do things and not just what we do relates to the ethics of the leader. The next section focuses on ethical leadership.

Ethical leadership

Due to ample corporate scandals, ethical leadership has gained much attention in the academic literature and popular press alike. Brown and Treviño (2006) describe **ethical leadership** as normatively appropriate behaviour based on a respect for ethical values and promotion of ethical conduct in others, through rewards and punishments. An article by Banks, Fisher, Gooty, and Stock (2021), in *The Leadership Quarterly*, offers a systematic review of ethical leadership and reveals that several definitions of this phenomenon include values as a consistent attribute. Many of these definitions refer to values that are focused on the interest of others. An ethical leader should thus possess caution and wisdom in making decisions that affect the future of others. Being an ethical leader requires courage during adversity, restraint, equitable behaviour, or justice. Ethical leaders thus behave in ways that benefit others and refrain from behaviours that would cause harm to others. Interestingly, Banks et al. (2021) apply Signal Theory to explain that ethical leaders send ethical signals via their behaviour to customers, suppliers, and even investors. These signals could include an ethical leader attending a charity event. However, since leadership is a social influencing process, Banks et al. (2021) observe that others need to notice the behaviour of the ethical leader to be influenced by it.

Ethical leadership distinguishes itself from other forms of moral leadership by placing emphasis on using rewards and punishments to ensure compliance (Metcalf & Benn, 2013). Ethical leadership and authentic leadership share their emphasis on honesty, openness, and integrity, whereas **authentic leadership** pays particular attention to being authentic or transparent in relationships.

In line with ethical leadership, the servant leader focuses on serving others. As discussed in Chapter 3, the servant leadership style therefore is intended to be beneficial to followers (Howell, 2013). Originally, Greenleaf (1977) defined **servant leadership** as the desire to serve others and a conscious choice to lead. The intention of servant leaders has been described more recently as growing others into servant leaders (Van Dierendonck, 2011). While there are differences among the forms of moral leadership, they are all relevant to counter the lack of ethical practices and ethical consciousness in business, which hinders economic development (Waldman, Siegel, & Stahl, 2020).

So far, we discussed strategic leadership and referred to ethical and servant leadership. The next section of this chapter focuses on developing the capabilities of leaders through various forms of leadership development.

Leadership development

In general, leadership development entails an individual who develops leadership skills. There are several methods that a person can employ to develop leadership skills, such as being exposed to other cultures. There are also leadership development programmes where individuals are purposefully exposed to new cultures, by traveling to new destinations. This exposure to unfamiliar places and cultures could challenge leaders to open their minds to how other people might view the world and how businesses are run in other settings. For some leaders, exposure comes through living abroad for a period and learning about different mindsets in this way. In other cases, leadership development programmes could entail immersions, where leaders are taken to places where they would not ordinarily visit, such as a poorer area in the inner city. After this visit, a debrief is usually facilitated where the participants in the programme share their experiences and the impression that the immersion made on them. The discussion that follows these immersions assists leaders in becoming more aware of their own value system and the value systems of their peers in the programme. They are often challenged to consider and reconsider their own world view during these discussions.

Another common method used in leadership development is to gather feedback from subordinates, peers, and the supervisor of the leader. Usually, respondents receive a questionnaire with questions on a

Likert-type scale. For example, some questions may include: "My leader is open to new ideas" and "My leader openly communicates with his/her team". The respondent must then answer on a five- point scale from 1 ("always like that") to 5 ("never like that"); those responses best correspond to their leader. This type of questionnaire is called a **360-degree feedback** questionnaire, since information is gathered from multiple individuals who work with the leader. The feedback from the respondents could then be displayed in graphs, showing how the different groups of people responded to the questions. In leadership development programmes, these 360-degree feedback questionnaires are often used to offer feedback and a debriefing process follows. In some settings, a facilitator will explain the implications of the feedback in a group format, or sometimes the debriefing will take place in a one-on-one setting, where an executive coach will give the feedback and facilitate a sense-making process with the leader.

In the case study referred to earlier in the chapter, AngloGold Ashanti namely uses the System for People framework in their leadership development (Boninelli, 2013), originally called the Stratified Systems Theory discussed in **Elliott Jacques's (1996)** book titled *Requisite Organisation: A total system for effective managerial organization and managerial leadership for the 21st century*. **The Stratified Systems Theory** holds that the different managerial levels in an organisation require different levels of complexity thinking. For example, the leaders need to focus on strategic thinking and be able to handle a variety of complex interrelated variables at the top of the organisation. On operational levels, leaders need to translate that strategy into operational goals and targets. AngloGold Ashanti focuses holistically to ensure that leaders are working at their current level of capability. Interaction is encouraged between leaders and followers regarding feedback on performance, leadership effectiveness, recognition, and coaching. This interaction must take place within a larger context where accountability and authority are clear.

Boninelli (2013) explains how AngloGold Ashanti builds its internal leadership talent pool. At AngloGold Ashanti, there is a focus on matching individual capability to role complexity. **Work complexity** means the complexity of decision-making required in a role. Complexity points to the number of variables, the interdependencies between them, the clarity with which they can be identified, and their rate of change. **Individual capability** entails the cognitive capacity to handle complexities associated with a specific role, as well as the actual ability of an individual to conduct decisions on a specific level of complexity. Given the individual leader's current capability, projection is then made of potential future capabilities. This projection is based on a scientific process linked to the Stratified Systems Theory of Elliott Jacques (1996). Based on these assessments, individual development plans are then drawn up.

Interestingly, AngloGold Ashanti uses the manager-once-removed from the individual leader to oversee the assessment of the individual leader. That is, the manager-once-removed is the manager of that leader's supervisor. This manager-once-removed plays a mentoring role for this individual manager. The direct manager of the individual leader receives on-the-job coaching on specific performance areas. The Human Resources division within AngloGold Ashanti plays a facilitating role in this process of assessing and developing the individual leader. Refer to the case study of Moore, Hawarden, and Scheepers (2019) for an example of how the talent management works at AngloGold Ashanti.

Anglo-Gold Ashanti is an excellent example which demonstrates the active involvement of the leader's organisation in leadership development. In most cases, the leader must actively seek opportunities to develop their own leadership skills. The implication for you is this: when your job responsibilities exceed your current capabilities, you might experience high levels of stress, anxiety, and even burnout. Within the first three months in a new position, you might experience these feelings; however, over time you should be in a position where you are more comfortable in your role. After a while, you might start experiencing boredom, which then might cause you to underperform. This is because the lack of challenge might cause you to be disinterested, since the issues that you need to deal with are too predictable to give you an adrenaline surge. The optimal position is to be in flow, which is the mix of being comfortable and confident, as well as being challenged, and feeling stretched and balanced; and being focused on your job. You might be so focused that you lose track of time, place, and experience being phased-out in a way. Refer to Csikszentmihalyi (2012) for a good illustration about being in flow with the positive psychology literature, which is a scientific approach to studying human thoughts, feelings, and behaviour, with a focus on strengths instead of weaknesses (Peterson, 2008).

Coaching

An important leadership development mechanism is coaching. Coaching offers leaders the thinking space or head-space to reflect and for carefully considering options. In this regard, Kline (2009) emphasises that the greatest gift we can offer each other is the framework in which to think for ourselves. Stout-Rostron (2014: 46) describes a coach as a thought partner for the leader, helping them to think clearly about the issues they need to address. The coaching conversation is "a thinking partnership, where coach and client reflect on the client's experience, transforming it into potential for learning and action". Business coaching is the broader term, whereas executive coaching is a subset involving leaders with positions at the executive level. The main difference between coaching and mentoring is that being directive or giving advice directly is closer to what a mentor would do than a coach.

Mentoring

Mentoring is a powerful tool to develop potential leaders' skills, help them build networks, increase career satisfaction, and expose them to opportunities (Ivey & Dupré, 2022). The mentor role theory of Kram (1985) offers a classic definition of **mentoring** as a relationship between a senior, more experienced person and a junior, less experienced person. The role of a mentor is to share their insight and to give advice to the leader from their own frame of reference or experience. Mentoring could also involve the mentor introducing the leader to their network. Sponsorship goes further and promotes the leader by "selling" the competencies of the leader to others, so that the leader could get access to opportunities and exposure to further the leader's career. Stout-Rostron (2014) advises that mentoring usually includes domain-specific expertise. A relevant question for you is, "Who has already achieved success in the area where you aspire to succeed?" You can ask this person to be your mentor and meet on a regular basis to learn from this person.

Organisational leadership and development in the African context

Leadership development in Africa is more important now than ever before. According to Gicheha Gitau, the senior principal and head of people analytics at Career Connections based out of Kenya, "Africa is a talent hub competing on a global scale...Organisations are realising the direct impact of leadership on employee engagement, productivity, diversity, and the overall organisational culture" (Hogan Assessments, 2023). Many organisations in Africa are investing in leadership development to train both new and experienced managers who can increase growth and build capacity (Eckert & Rweyongoza, 2015). Due to the shortage of emerging leaders, the demand for effective leadership and its systematic development is rapidly growing. Based on data collected in Egypt, West Africa (Ghana, Nigeria, Benin, Togo, Guinea, Niger, Burkina Faso), and Southern Africa (South Africa, Botswana, Namibia), the development of critical skills is imperative in the following areas:

- Leading diverse teams
- Adaptability in the workplace
- Vulnerability and reflection in development areas
- Transferability of knowledge and coaching subordinates

- Collaboration and communication
- Building employee engagement
- Coping with complexity

In the following section, we showcase an example of how education and training supported the leadership growth of Zimbabwean-born Tongesai Chingwena (also known as TC). The following excerpt was taken from the personal account of his educational journey (from an interview conducted in 2023), where he further expands on the vital role that his agency played in establishing and leading businesses in Africa's challenging climate:

> While completing my undergraduate degree in BSc. Hons. Electrical Engineering in the year 2000, I founded a new venture, Frolgate Technology Pvt. Ltd. The venture was founded on the need to address some market gaps arising from a computer technology crisis popularly known as the Y2K Bug. At that time, this technology crisis led to a massive market transition and institutional pivot in the Information and Communication Technology (ICT) ICT domain. Although the venture formally registered two years later, I discovered that the first two years of the business were much more difficult than writing an executable computer code I had learnt in my fourth year. Understanding the unpredictable behaviour of the market, assembling a team, building a customer base, and accessing financing options whilst competing against established incumbents was more difficult than I ever imagined.
>
> With some 15 years of experience running this venture, I embarked on diversifying into the healthcare industry. In 2016, I founded Utano Africa Healthcare, a new venture focused on providing tech-based solutions in imaging and diagnostics for healthcare professionals. Thinking that my experience was going to count much, I was surprised that the problems I faced in the year 2000 were even more visible and bigger this time. This is an industry that is heavily regulated, requiring higher financing, formalisation and compliance, and a greater awareness of ethics.
>
> During my MPhil studies with the Gordon Institute of Business Science at the University of Pretoria in 2018, I was alerted to the notion of value-creating mechanisms in the Strategic Management and Strategic Leadership courses. After studying many case studies during the courses, I got to understand the need for leadership mentalities that would suggest having an export-oriented unit within a business portfolio. With this enlightenment, I founded TechBank Africa in 2019, with a focus on the extractive industry, starting with gold mining and processing, and further pursuing gas

exploration opportunities. With mining being in an industry category with so many dependencies, regulations and high capital intensity, the formative years have been extremely challenging. A key and consistent activity in all these ventures has been to engage potential customers, investors, banks and regulatory bodies during which my team and I pitched our profiles, ideas and our experience so as to gain access to multiple stakeholder resources across multiple countries.

My doctoral study is inspired by the need to understand how new ventures in a largely informal economy like Zimbabwe navigate conflicting legitimacy judgements so as to access resources for survival.

Tongesai Chingwena (2023). Read more about Frolgate Technology Group here: https://www.frolgategroup.co.zw

The interview with Tongesai Chingwena reveals the challenges which organisational leaders in Africa face and how his educational journey has assisted him with insights to establish new businesses and to maintain those businesses over time.

Conclusion

In this chapter, we focused on organisational leadership and the strategic leadership competencies required to lead at this level of complexity. We shared a couple of examples of organisations who shared a vision throughout the organisation and which focused on people's capabilities. We discussed the different levels of leadership development programmes and the focus areas of these training programmes.

Discussion questions

- Discuss the importance of strategic leadership in your organisation and/or school.
- With respect to strategic leadership, how is the alignment between strategic intent and business performance in your organisation and/or school?
- Discuss the importance of developing a "net positive" or sustainability vision in Africa.
- What are the key trends related to strategic leadership for the 21st century in Africa?
- Which leadership development approaches do you prefer? Why?
- Are certain leadership development approaches more effective on the African continent? Why?

Exercises

Exercise 1: Balanced Scorecard exercise

The Balanced Scorecard is a powerful tool to ensure that a clear strategy map and strategic objectives are aligned across the business units internal to the organisation. Using Figure 6.1 in this chapter, reflect on your own company and/or school. Respond to the questions in the figure of the Balanced Scorecard. Based on your responses, are there any gaps? What are your next steps?

Exercise 2: Reflection essay exercise

In this chapter, we discussed organisational leadership and development, which focuses on both the organisation and individual. After reflecting on the questions below, write a 500-word essay. As an organisation:

- Are we considering the future customers' needs, in addition to our current ones?
- Would we rather suffer than change?
- Would we buy what we sell?
- Do we do good through our business operations or are we somehow harming the environment and the communities around our business or maybe even our own employees?

As an individual:

- How much flow are you experiencing at the moment in your current position?

(A reminder: Flow means that there is a balance between the responsibilities that you need to carry and the level of capability you have to meet these challenges)

- Who has already achieved success in the area in which you want to achieve and whom you could ask to mentor you?

References

Banks, G. C., Fisher, T., Gooty, J., & Stock, G. (2021). Ethical leadership: Mapping the terrain for concept cleanup and a future research agenda. *The Leadership Quarterly*, *32*, 101471. https://doi.org/10.1016/j.leaqua.2020.101471

Beer, M., Voelpel, S., Leibold, M., & Tekie, E. (2005). Strategic management as organizational learning: Developing fit and alignment through a disciplined process, *Long Range Planning*, *38*(5), 445–465.

Boal, K. B., & Hooijberg, R. (2001). Strategic leadership research: Moving on. *Leadership Quarterly*, *11*, 515–549.

Boninelli, I. (2013). Global talent management case study: Talent management in AngloGold Ashanti. In S. Bluen (Ed.), *Talent Management in emerging markets* (Chapter 10, pp. 231–258). Randburg: Knowres.

Brown, M. E., & Treviño, L. K. (2006). Ethical leadership: A review and future directions. *The Leadership Quarterly*, *17*, 595–616.

Carter, S. M., & Greer, C. R. (2013). Strategic leadership: Values, styles and organizational performance. *Journal of Leadership & Organizational Studies*, *20*(4), 375–393. https://doi.org/10.1177/1548051812471724

Chingwena, T. (2023). Personal interview with authors during Tongesai Chingwena's Masters and Doctoral studies at the Gordon Institute of Business Science, University of Pretoria.

Csikszentmihalyi, M. (2012). How can we become more engaged with work? Concept of flow. In S. Cantore & J. Passmore (Eds.), *Top business psychology models: 50 transforming ideas for leaders, consultants and coaches* (pp. 13–16). London: KoganPage.

Eckert, R., & Rweyongoza, S. (2015). Leadership development in Africa: A focus on strengths. *The Center for Creative Leadership, December*. Retrieved from https://cclinnovation.org/wp-content/uploads/2020/02/leadershipdevelopmentafrica.pdf

Greenleaf, R. K. (1977). *Servant leadership: A journey into the nature of legitimate power and greatness*. Mahwah, NJ: Paulist Press.

Hitt, M. A., Haynes, K. T., & Serpa, R. (2010). Strategic leadership for the 21st century. *Business Horizons*, *53*, 437–444.

Hogan Assessments (2023). Leadership in Africa: The past, present, and future Posted. *Hogan Assessments*. Retrieved July 31, 2023, from https://www.hoganassessments.com/blog/leadership-in-africa/

Hooiberg, R., & Lane, N. (2014). Strategic leadership. In C. L. Cooper (Ed.), *Wiley encyclopedia of management*: *Vol. 12. Strategic management* (pp. 1–4). John Wiley and Sons. https://doi.org/10.1002/9781118785317.weom120215

Hough, J., Thompson, A. A., Stickland III, A. J., & Gamble, J. (2008). *Crafting and executing strategy* (South African Edition). Berkshire, UK: McGraw-Hill Education.

Howell, J. P. (2013). *Snapshots of great leadership*. Hove, England: Routledge.

Ivey, G. W., & Dupré, K. E. (2022). Workplace mentorship: A critical review. *Journal of Career Development*, *49*(3), 714–729. https://doi.org/10.1177/0894845320957737

Jacques, E. (1996). *Requisite organization: A total system for effective managerial organization and managerial leadership for the 21st century*. Arlington, Virginia: Cason Hall & Co.

Kaplan, R. S., & Norton, D. P. (1992). The Balanced Scorecard: Measures that drive performance. *Harvard Business Review*, *70*(1), 71–79.
Kaplan, R. S., & Norton, D. P. (2006). *Alignment. Using the balanced scorecard to create corporate synergies*. Boston, MA: Harvard Business Review Press.
Kline, N. (2009). *More time to think: A way of being in the world*. Pool-in-Wharfedale, England: Fisher King.
Kram, K. E. (1985). *Mentoring at work*. Glenview, IL: Scott, Foresman.
Osborn, R. N., & Marion, R. (2009). Contextual leadership, transformational leadership and the performance of international innovation seeking alliances. *The Leadership Quarterly*, *20*, 191–206.
Peterson, C. (2008). What is positive psychology, and what is it not? *Psychology Today*. https://www.psychologytoday.com/us/blog/the-good-life/200805/what-is-positive-psychology-and-what-is-it-not
Porter, L. W., & McLaughlin, G. B. (2006). Leadership and the organizational context: Like the weather? *Leadership Quarterly*, *17*, 559–576.
Metcalf, L., & Benn, S. (2013). Leadership for sustainability: An evolution of leadership ability. *Journal of Business Ethics*, *112*(3), 369–384.
Moore, A., Hawarden, V., & Scheepers, C. B. (2019). *Anglo American South Africa: Strategically mining leadership talent for succession*. Ivey Publishing. Case number: 9B19C004, https://www.iveypublishing.ca/s/product/anglo-american-south-africa-strategically-mining-leadership-talent-for-succession/01t5c00000CwojDAAR
Nadkarni, S., & Narayanan, V. K. (2007). Strategic schemas, strategic flexibility, and firm performance: The moderating role of industry clock speed. *Strategic Management Journal*, *28*, 234–270. https://doi.org/10.1002/smj.576
Scheepers, C. B., Verachia, A., & Motsepe, S. (2018). *T-Systems South Africa: Contextual leadership of shared value* (Case No. 9B18C024). Ivey Publishing.
Stobierski, T. (2021). What is corporate social responsibility? 4 types. *Harvard Business School Online*. Retrieved April 8, 2021, from https://online.hbs.edu/blog/post/types-of-corporate-social-responsibility
Stout-Rostron, S. (2014). *Leadership coaching for results: Cutting-edge practices for coach and client*. Randburg: Knowres.
Tawse, A., & Tabesh, P. (2021). Strategy implementation: A review and an introductory framework. *European Management Journal*, *39*(1), 22–33. https://doi.org/10.1016/j.emj.2020.09.005
Van Dierendonck, D. (2011). Servant leadership: A review and synthesis. *Journal of Management*, *37*, 1228–1261.
Waldman, D. A., Siegel, D. S., & Stahl, G. K. (2020). Defining the socially responsible leader: Revisiting issues in responsible leadership. *Journal of Leadership & Organizational Studies*, *27*(1), 5–20. https://doi.org/10.1177/1548051819872201
World Economic Forum (2023). Tony O. Elumelu: Chairman, UBA Group. https://www.weforum.org/people/tony-o-elumelu

7 The future of leadership in Africa

Chapter summary

This chapter discusses the future of leadership in Africa and highlights the key leadership issues and trends of the African continent. We discuss the importance of multicultural leadership, women in leadership, and the role of value-based leadership. Finally, the chapter examines the potential for African unity in the future of the African continent.

Learning objectives

After studying this chapter, you should be able to do the following:

- Discuss the key leadership issues and trends that impact the future of leadership in Africa.
- Identify aspects of multicultural leadership.
- Explain the contribution of women leaders.
- Recognise the importance of value-based leadership.
- Understand the potential of African unity and shared *Ubuntu* values for leadership in the 21st century.

Resson Kantai Duff, a community conservation advocate, is Deputy Director of Ewase Lions, an organisation dedicated to promoting coexistence between people and lions in northern Kenya. Prior to her involvement with the Ewase Lions, she was Head of Awareness at Save the Elephants and a writer and editor for the International Institute for Sustainable Development – Reporting Services. Duff's passion focuses on deconstructing the current narrative of conservation which has separated people from nature (National Geographic, 2023). Duff notes:

> The world has lost 68% of its wildlife populations in under 50 years, and there are people around the world working to protect and grow

DOI: 10.4324/9781003020523-7

> the wildlife that is left. In Africa, however, the approach for conserving this wildlife has almost always involved a separation of people from nature; the involvement from local people, but never leadership from the local people, and the problem statement that has often come from outside our continent.
>
> (TEDWomen, 2021)

Rather than the current approach for conservation, which has usually been led by "parachute conservationists" (outsiders who believe that they have all the answers and hire locals to implement them and then disappear), Duff advocates for community-led conservation (Management Skills for Wildlife Conservation, MSWC, 2023)—that is, locals leading these efforts themselves with a focus on indigenous local leadership. Duff argues:

> If we do not change this (parachute conservationists) approach to conservation of Africa, we will lose all our wildlife, and with it, a part of our humanity. I believe that the time for Africans to define conservation ourselves has come. And when Africa leads its own conservation efforts, we will not only restore our wildlife populations but our land, and our cultures, and our broken relationship with nature.
>
> (TEDWomen, 2021)

Our final chapter discusses the key leadership issues and trends impacting the future of Africa, including sustainable management and conservation. The chapter then examines multicultural leadership and women in leadership, such as Resson Kantai Duff. We finally discuss the role of value-based leadership and the potential for African unity in the future of the African continent.

Leadership issues and trends impacting the future of Africa

Future leaders in Africa will be required to tackle central challenges in today's changing technological, economic, and social landscapes and redefine leadership. According to Professor Reshad Jaumally, Chairman of YKBS (Youth Kinetic and Business Society) in Mauritius, an African vision for leadership for the 21st century focuses on the following areas:

- Equality and inclusion: African leaders need to prepare for the negative effects of rapid economic growth, including environmental degradation and the increasing divide between the "haves" and the "have-nots". Inclusion is needed for opportunity and innovation to succeed across the continent.

- Leadership with ethics: African leaders need to have a strong clarity of their personal values and lead their communities through value-based leadership.
- An African approach: African leaders need to draw from their pre-colonial heritage, history, and creativity to develop strategies that fit their unique characteristics and requirements rather than relying solely on Western-based leadership models.

(Jaumally, 2023)

An African vision is particularly crucial given the current predictions, suggesting that by 2030, one in five people in the world will be African. While this may be surprising, half the continent's population is already under the age of 20, and all ten of the world's youngest countries are in Africa. As a result, one can expect a large workforce in Africa for the next several decades and a significant pool of potential future leaders to serve at all levels, from local community to international (Jaumally, 2023). In contrast, Preston and Stokes (2012) explain that the populations of developed countries are aging.

Due to these projections, Fred Swaniker, a Ghanaian serial entrepreneur, aims to develop three million educated African leaders in politics, business, and healthcare and education by 2035. Swaniker established his "leadership university" across the continent with the goal of transforming the world's largest and youngest workforce (Richardson, 2019). Given projections that by 2100, the African continent could account for 40% of the world's births, Swaniker notes, "Imagine 40% of the world's population without opportunity … We're not only going to have an African crisis- it's a global crisis" (Richardson, 2019). To develop leaders capable of driving the continent forward, Swaniker founded the African Leadership University, a school where entrepreneurship is a core subject, and students select missions rather than majors, such as building a business for bamboo coal or understanding elephant movement patterns in the Serengeti.

Swaniker views the conservation industry as a "low-hanging fruit" for entrepreneurial Africans. Aligning with Resson Kantai Duff's perspective in the introductory case in this chapter, Swaniker argues, "No change in Africa will happen when it's driven by Westerners" (Richardson, 2019). Specifically, it is important to have African-centred conservancy management leadership education. For example, MSWC's Leadership and Management Programme (LAMP) partnered with Northern Rangelands Trust (supporting 39 community conservancies across northern and coastal Kenya) to offer community-based leadership and management training to women from Lekurruki and Il Ngwesi community conservancies.

Another big challenge to Africa's development is accountable leadership, according to Signé (2019), senior fellow in the Global Economy and Development Program and the African Growth Initiative at the Brookings Institute. There is growing hope that the next generation of youth will play a central role in building accountability for successful economic transformation, representation, and public service. The youths need to take leadership positions in the council of ministries, parliaments, national committees, corporate boardrooms, and civil society organisational teams (Signé, 2019).

Once young leaders hold positions of influence, they can build strong institutions for accountability and educate people about the importance of accountability for a successful continent. Youth leaders can advance civil society growth, poverty reduction, economic expansion, and innovation by strengthening the participation of women and youth, endorsing human rights, access to justice, and ensuring inclusion of all communities (Signé, 2019). In the next section, we discuss the role of multicultural leadership in building an inclusive workplace culture in Africa.

Multicultural leadership

A **multicultural leader** possesses the skills and attitudes to relate effectively to and motivate people across race, gender, age, social attitudes, and lifestyles (DuBrin, 2019). Cultural differences are generalisations and serve as a starting point for a leader to interact with people. Given Africa's rich cultural diversity in distinct languages and tribes (Britannica, 2023), leaders should be sensitive to their subordinates' cultural differences.[1] As discussed in Chapter 1, Hofstede's national cultural dimensions and the GLOBE project of several African countries provide frameworks for understanding these cultural differences and help leaders in a culturally diverse workplace. In particular, leaders must recognise the individual differences of those employees who live outside of their native country, who are generally called expatriates, as they may or may not adhere to their home country's cultural values and practices and may take on the values of the new host country. Leaders must be sensitive to these individual differences and take care to understand each person's preferences, rather than assuming them.

Leaders building an inclusive workplace must be alert to cultural differences and show sensitivity and willingness to learn about others' cultural orientations and values. DuBrin (2019: 373) explains, "a cross-cultural leader must be patient, adaptable, flexible and willing to listen and learn". Cultural sensitivity includes curiosity about why people of another culture act as they do. For example, the importance of punctuality in arriving at work and scheduled meetings could cause cultural misunderstandings. Leaders should, therefore, be specific about deadlines of assignments.

In sum, leaders dedicated to building an inclusive workplace must focus on cultural diversity. Another element of diversity that is relevant to leadership in the African context is women's leadership. Next, we discuss the importance of striving for gender equality, the current status of gender equality, the possible reasons for the lack of women leaders in senior positions, and some proposed solutions to the issue.

Women leaders

Karabo Morule is an example of an African female leader who reached an executive position in a male-dominated business. A teaching case study about the culture change that she led at Old Mutual is one of the best-selling cases on the Harvard Publishing platform for African cases. Karabo was one of the first Black African actuaries in South Africa. In her leadership, Karabo was purposefully inclusive and ensured that employees were engaged. She purposefully unleashed the energy in people on the African continent and was passionate about people's development. Read more about Morule's leadership of culture change at Old Mutual in Govender and Scheepers (2020).

Despite the importance of gender equality, progress has been slow. A recent report from the World Economic Forum estimates that women will not attain parity with men for another 131 years, not until 2154 (Wallace, 2023). The European Union argues that the lack of women in leadership positions means that female talent is underutilised, human capital is wasted, and the quality of appointments to the highest positions may be compromised. As of 2023, Sub-Saharan Africa has closed 68.2% of its gender gap, meaning that females are, on the average, approximately 32% less likely to have the same opportunities as males. It should be noted that there are large differences from a country perspective. Namibia, South Africa, and Rwanda had the best results, with an index of approximately 0.8 (an average gender gap of around 20%), while Chad had the lowest performance, with a score of 0.57 (Galal, 2023).

The number of high-ranking women in Africa is limited. A McKinsey and Company (2022) report indicates that women accounted for only 5% of chief executive officers (CEOs) in Africa in 2017. Scheepers, Douman, and Moodley (2018) suggest that women in leadership introduce open communication and diverse perspectives, benefitting the organisation.

Hoobler, Masterson, Nkomo, and Michel's (2018) meta-analysis confirms the notion that the presence of women leadership, specifically a female CEO, has a positive impact on the organisation's ability to generate revenues and overall performance. Similarly, Scholtz and Kieviet (2018) found that the top 100 South African companies with significant female representation on their boards of directors achieved 5.4% higher growth in market returns than other listed companies with fewer women represented.

What are the possible causes for gender inequality? Research suggests that the lack of perceived value of women's leadership revolves around gender stereotyping, attributions, unconscious bias, and a lack of role models (Koenig, Eagly, Mitchell, & Ristikari, 2011). First, most people hold stereotypes of men as having more leadership characteristics than women. Fortunately, this tendency has decreased over time (Koenig et al., 2011).

A factor that contributes to gender inequality is unconscious bias. Unconscious or implicit bias implies that a person consciously rejects stereotypes; however, they unconsciously evaluate others based on stereotypes (Hill, Miller, Benson, & Handley, 2016). Thus, implicit biases are unintentional beliefs or attitudes that inform unconscious actions and decisions. This bias remains a barrier for women to advance to top leadership positions (Shelby-Rosette, Koval, Ma, & Livingston, 2016).

What are some possible solutions to gender inequality in the workplace? Leaders must work to close the gender gaps in career advancement and eliminate workplace discrimination. Concrete ways include transparent salaries, flexible work options, and training opportunities for women (Wooll, 2021). Additionally, we can all make a meaningful impact to eliminate gender inequality by recognising our own unconscious biases and recognising the value of more inclusive organisations.

With the increasing number of organisations focusing on changing their organisational culture to be more inclusive, it is expected that there will be more equal opportunities for women and men in the workplace in Africa. For example, Unilever's Sunlight Women of More programme is designed to empower women and help address the imbalance of women in East African business. In collaboration with the United Nations Institute for Training and Research (UNITAR), Sunlight's Women of More Programme empowers women entrepreneurs through financial literacy training and plans to reach over 100,00 women in East Africa by the end of 2026 with their new partnership with Absa Bank of Kenya (Unilever, 2023). The Global School Business Network (GBSN), a network of the world's leading business schools, also partnered with Ecobank to launch the Ellevate Leadership Training Program to serve and nurture the success of women-owned and women-led businesses by developing their leadership skills. Its initial cohort were from ten African countries: Cameroon, Ghana, Kenya, Liberia, Malawi, Nigeria, Sierra Leone, Uganda, Zambia, and Zimbabwe (GBSN, 2023).

Value-based leadership

A value-based leadership perspective is crucial for the future of leadership in Africa. Values-based leadership encompasses both a leadership style and a philosophy based on the shared beliefs and assumptions of the leader and the team. This set of shared values fosters alignment within teams and enhances productivity (Falcone, 2022). A key characteristic of value-based leadership is its selflessness. Value-based leadership behaviours include styles that have a moral, authentic, and ethical dimension (Copeland, 2014). Given that corruption remains a significant issue affecting the African continent (Economist, 2020), it's important for African leaders to lead their communities using value-based leadership. As discussed in Chapter 1, the prevalence of corruption on the continent deprives millions of Africans of their basic needs such as food, health, and education.

Moreover, value-based leadership serves as the foundation for a leader's commitment to sustainability. According to Banerji and Maitra (2022), the ability for change initiatives to align with various Sustainable Development Goals (SDGs) hinges on senior leaders who are driven by values and fully committed to sustainability. Sustainability-driven businesses prioritise caring over mere financial considerations. This commitment to sustainability is often seen in the concept of the **triple bottom line**, which emphasises profit, people, and the planet (Perrot, 2015). Leaders must assess the extent to which their companies prioritise the well-being of people and the planet alongside profit. However, van Prooijen and Ellemers (2015) suggest that many organisations prioritise profit over ethics, sometimes even compromising their moral principles for financial gain. More recently, African countries have agreed to increase their commitment and work hard at achieving SDGs, especially those goals that aim to end poverty and hunger as outlined by the Food and Agriculture Organisation (FAO) of the United Nations (2023). The countries welcomed the FAO's Four Betters strategic framework 2022–2023 which shapes the organisation's work for better production, better nutrition, a better environment, and a better life for all, leaving no one behind. In addition, Africa's youths have also pledged to work harder to achieve its SDG goals by 2030 (UNECA, 2022).

African unity and values

Jaumally (2023) noted that an African approach is needed for an African vision of leadership for the 21st century. According to Lerutla and Steyn (2021), African business leadership consists of eight elements: (1) leadership seen as unique to leaders on the continent (Afrocentric); (2) leadership as an act of service to the community (*Ubuntu*- "I am because we are"); (3) leadership principles operating in challenging and resource-deprived environments (because of the legacy of colonialism); (4) leadership providing hope for creating a better future; (5) leaders being dominated by those in positions of (political) authority; (6) leaders who engage in entrepreneurial activities; and yet (7) leaders as still requiring development because many leaders are corrupt (brokenness); and (8) leadership which seems to be legitimised by post-colonial sentiments (Afro-centric). In particular, Lerutla and Steyn's (2021) research highlights the importance of *Ubuntu* in leadership. As discussed in Chapter 1, *Ubuntu* also resembles *Umoja* (togetherness). Khoza (2012) explains that the humane style of leadership generated by African humanism puts people first and that leadership represents a meeting of spirits between individuals and communities.

Galperin, Lituchy, and Punnett (2017) also consider the importance of the Agenda 2063 for the future for the African continent and creating African unity. Agenda 2063 is Africa's 50-year roadmap, which outlines "a global strategy to optimise the use of Africa's resources for the benefit of all Africans" (African Union, 2016). It is an element of the African Renaissance, which promotes changes in attitudes, and mindsets to instil the right set of African values, including discipline, focus, honesty, integrity, transparency, hard work, and love for Africa and its people. Agenda 2063 strives to promote a high degree of productivity, growth, entrepreneurship, and transformation within the African continent. Galperin et al. (2017) refer to the Agenda 2063 of the African Union as an important transformative vision and argue that the implementation of Agenda 2063 requires effective leadership, which is based on a paradigm of African values and culture.

All in all, there is a bright future for Africa. Jaumally (2023) argues, "technologically savvy, innovation-hungry, cosmopolitan youth" will "harnesses the 4IR[2]" (also called the Fourth Industrial Revolution) and "propel the continent into a new, empowered future as it steps out onto the world stage". In addition, the increasing proportion of young African entrepreneurs who are especially committed to sustainability will continue to lead our communities. Nevertheless, for the next generation of leaders to thrive, it is especially important that they return to their pre-colonial heritage and draw upon African concepts, such as *Ubuntu* and *Umoja*. In addition, African leaders need to view inclusion as an opportunity to succeed across the continent and adopt a value-based leadership style, which has a moral, authentic, and ethical dimension.

Conclusion

Future leaders in Africa will need to adopt a transformative approach that embraces inclusion, ethical leadership, and an Afrocentric vision. Leaders like Resson Kantai Duff exemplify the potential of community-driven initiatives to restore both ecosystems and cultural ties, emphasizing the need for local leadership in conservation. Multicultural leadership and the advancement of women in leadership are essential to building diverse and inclusive workplaces that reflect Africa's rich cultural heritage and potential. A focus on value-based leadership and sustainability is equally critical, especially given the continent's unique challenges and opportunities. Lastly, the philosophy of *Ubuntu* and frameworks like Agenda 2063 highlight the significance of unity and shared values in planning for a prosperous, sustainable future for Africa.

Discussion Questions

- How can African leaders effectively address the challenges of economic inequality and environmental degradation while fostering innovation and opportunity across the continent?
- With Africa's youthful population, what strategies can be employed to develop the next generation of accountable and effective leaders?
- What are the advantages and potential challenges of community-led conservation initiatives in Africa, such as those advocated by Resson Kantai Duff?
- What specific policies or initiatives can African organizations adopt to close gender gaps in career advancement and leadership?
- What are some ways African leaders can balance profit, people, and the planet in their organizational strategies?
- What are the critical components of Agenda 2063, and how can leaders promote African unity and development through its initiatives?

Exercise 1: Women in leadership

Think of a female leader that you admire. After writing down the name of this person, answer the following questions:

- What are the traits and behaviours that make this person a great leader?
- How does this person make you feel?
- What are the outcomes of this leader's performance?
- Does the person embrace African traditions?
- Is the person motivated to attain the United Nation's (UN's) sustainable development goals?
- Does the person care about conserving natural resources?
- How might you best support this female leader?

Notes

1 Refer to Statista (2023) for a cultural diversity index score in Africa as of 2023, by leading country.
2 The 4IR is the next phase in the digitisation of the manufacturing sector, which will be powered by disruptive trends, such as the

increase of data and connectivity, analytics, human-machine interaction, and improvements in robotics (McKinsey & Company, 2022).

References

African Union. (2016). Agenda 2063 vision and priorities. *African Union*. Retrieved from http://agenda2063.au.int/en/vision

Banerji, B., & Maitra, P. (2022). Connecting value-based leadership to sustainability in India. In T. Sharma, R. Sinha Ray, & N. Mitra (Eds.), *Responsible leadership for sustainability in uncertain times. Responsible leadership and sustainable management*. Singapore: Springer. https://doi.org/10.1007/978-981-19-4723-0_10

Britannica. (2023). Africa cultural patterns. *Britannica*. https://www.britannica.com/place/Africa/Cultural-patterns

Copeland, M. K. (2014). The emerging significance of values-based leadership: A literature review. *International Journal of Leadership Studies*, *8*, 105–135.

Dubrin, A. J. (2019). *Leadership. Research findings, practice and skills*. Boston, MA: Cengage.

Economist. (2020). Africa is changing so rapidly, it is becoming hard to ignore. Special Report.

Falcone, P. (2022). Values-based leadership in action. *SHRM Newsletter*. Retrieved June 9, 2022, from https://www.shrm.org/resourcesandtools/hr-topics/employee-relations/pages/values-based-leadership-in-action.aspx#:~:text=Values%2Dbased%20leadership%20is%20both,and%20benefit%20from%20higher%20productivity

Galal, S. (2023). Gender gap in Sub-Saharan Africa 2023, by country. *Statista*. Retrieved September 22, 2023, from https://www.statista.com/statistics/1220485/gender-gap-index-in-sub-saharan-africa-by-country/

Galperin, B. L., Lituchy, T. R., & Punnett, B. J. (2017). The new frontier in the birthplace of mankind: Some conclusions and future directions. In T. R. Lituchy, B. L. Galperin, & B. J. Punnett (Eds.), *LEAD: Leadership Effectiveness in Africa and the African Diaspora* (pp. 237–250). New York: Palgrave McMillan.

Govender, M., & Scheepers, C. B. (2020). *Old mutual limited: Leading culture change*. Ivey Publishing. (Case No. 9B20C016).

GBSN (2023). Ellevate Leadership Training Program. Retrieved from https://gbsn.org/ellevate-leadership-training-program/

Hill, C., Miller, K., Benson, K., & Handley, G. (2016). *Barriers and bias: The status of women in leadership*. American Association of University Women. Retrieved from https://www.ncgs.org/wp-content/uploads/2017/11/Barriers-and-Bias-The-Status-of-Women-in-Leadership.pdf

Hoobler, J. M., Masterson, C. R., Nkomo, S. M., & Michel, E. J. (2018). The business case for women leaders: Meta-analysis, research critique, and path forward. *Journal of Management*, *44*(6), 2473–2499. https://doi.org/10.1177%2F0149206316628643

Jaumally, R. J. (2023). Leadership for the 21st century. *Honoris*. Retrieved from https://honoris.net/leadership-for-the-21st-century-an-african-vision/

Koenig, A. M., Eagly, A. H., Mitchell, A. A., & Ristikari, T. (2011). Are Leaders stereotypes masculine? A meta-analysis of three research paradigms. *Psychological Bulletin*, *137*(4), 616–642. https://doi.apa.org/doi/10.1037/a0023557

Khoza, R. J. (2012). The Ubuntu philosophy as a conceptual framework for interpersonal relationships and leadership. Address by Dr Reuel J. Khoza, Chairman of Nedbank Group Limited, to the Nedbank Group Technology Leaders. Retrieved from www.reuelkhoza.co.za/ubuntu-philosophy-conceptual-framework-interpersonalrelationships-leadership

Lerutla, M., & Steyn, R. (2021). African business leadership: Perspectives from aspiring young leaders. *South African Journal of Human Resource Management*, 19(0), a1467. https://doi.org/10.4102/sajhrm.v19i0.1467

McKinsey & Company (2022). What are Industry 4.0, the Fourth Industrial Revolution, and 4IR? Retrieved August 17, 2022, from https://www.mckinsey.com/featured-insights/mckinsey-explainers/what-are-industry-4-0-the-fourth-industrial-revolution-and-4ir

MSWC (2023). Management skills for Wildlife Conservation. https://mswconline.org/

National Geographic (2023). Resson Kantai Duff. https://explorer-directory.nationalgeographic.org/resson-kantai-duff

Perrot, E. (2015). Building the sustainable organization: An integrated approach. *Journal of Business Strategy*, *36*(1), 41–51.

Richardson, H. (2019). Why the next wave of leaders is African. Retrieved August 26, 2019, from https://www.bbc.com/worklife/article/20190826-why-the-next-wave-of-leaders-is-african

Preston, S. H., & Stokes, A. (2012). Sources of population aging in more and less developed countries. *Population Development Rev*, *National Library of Medicine*, *38*(2), 221–236. https://www.ncbi.nlm.nih.gov/pmc/articles/PMC3957219/

Scheepers, C. B., Douman, A., & Moodley, P. (2018). Sponsorship and social identity in advancement of women leaders in South Africa. *Gender in Management: An International Journal*, *33*(6), 466–498. https://doi.org/10.1108/GM-06-2017-0076

Scholtz, H., & Kieviet, S. (2018). The influence of board diversity on company performance of South African companies. *Journal of African Business*, *19*(1), 105–123. https://www.tandfonline.com/doi/full/10.1080/15228916.2017.1356065

Shelby-Rosette, A., Koval, C. Z., Ma, A., & Livingston, R. (2016). Race matters for women leaders: Intersectional effects on agentic deficiencies and penalties. *The Leadership Quarterly*, *27*(3), 429–445. https://doi.org/10.1016/j.leaqua.2016.01.008

Signé, L. (2019). Africa youth leadership: Building local leaders to solve global challenges. *Brookings*. Retrieved March 27, 2019, from https://www.brookings.edu/articles/africa-youth-leadership-building-local-leaders-to-solve-global-challenges/

Statista (2023). Cultural diversity index score in Africa as of 2023, by leading country. https://www.statista.com/statistics/1284654/most-diverse-countries-in-africa/

TEDWomen (2021). Why Africa needs community-led conservation. *Resson Kantai Duff*. Retrieved December 2021, from https://www.ted.com/talks/resson_kantai_duff_why_africa_needs_community_led_conservation?language=en

UNECA (2022). Young people in Africa have pledged to work harder and ensure that the continent achieves its Sustainable Development Goals (SDGs) by 2030. *Africa Renewal*. Retrieved January 2022, from https://www.un.org/africarenewal/magazine/january-2022/africa%E2%80%99s-youth-renew-commitment-sdgs

Unilever (2023). Sunlight Women of More: Empowering entrepreneurs. Retrieved from https://www.unilever.com/planet-and-society/equity-diversity-and-inclusion/promoting-diverse-suppliers/

United Nations (2023). Gender equality. The Sustainable Development Goals Report 2023. https://www.un.org/sustainabledevelopment/gender-equality/

van Prooijen, A.-M., & Ellemers, N. (2015). Does it pay to be moral? How indicators of morality and competence enhance organizational and work team attractiveness. *British Journal of Management*, *26*(2), 225–236. https://doi.org/10.1111/1467-8551.12055

Wallace, A. (2023). It could take 131 years for the world to close the gender gap, report shows. *CNN Business*. Retrieved June 20, 2023, from https://www.cnn.com/2023/06/20/economy/wef-global-gender-gap/index.html

Wooll, M. (2021). Gender inequality in the workplace: the fight against bias. *Better Up*. Retrieved October 15, 2021, from https://www.betterup.com/blog/gender-inequality-in-the-work-place

Index

Pages in *italics* refer to figures and pages in **bold** refer to tables.

Kolibri 360 GmbH
Ferdinand-Jühlke-Straße 7
99095 Erfurt, Deutschland
produktsicherheit@kolibri360.de